2004

THE BEST 10-MINUTE PLAYS
FOR THREE OR MORE ACTORS

Smith and Kraus's
Short Plays and 10-Minute Plays Collections

Christopher Durang Vol. I: 27 Short Plays

Frank D. Gilroy Vol. II: 15 One-Act Plays

Israel Horovitz Vol. I: 16 Short Plays

Romulus Linney 17 Short Plays

Terrence McNally Vol. I: 15 Short Plays

Lanford Wilson: 21 Short Plays

Act One Festival The Complete One-Act Plays: '95

Act One Festival The Complete One-Act Plays '94

EST Marathon The Complete One-Act Plays:

EST Marathon The Complete One-Act Plays: '98

EST Marathon The Complete One-Act Plays: '97

EST Marathon The Complete One-Act Plays: '96

EST Marathon The Complete One-Act Plays: '95

EST Marathon The Complete One-Act Plays: '94

HB Playwrights Short Play Festival

> 2003 The Subway Plays

> 2002 The Beach Plays

> 2001 The Hospital Plays

> 2000 The Funeral Plays

> 1999 The Airport Plays

> 1998 The Museum Plays

> 1997 The Motel Plays

Twenty One-Acts from 20 Years at the Humana Festival 1975–1995

The Women's Project and Productions Rowing to America and Sixteen Other Short Plays

8 TENS @ 8 Festival: 30 10-Minute Plays from the Santa Cruz Festivals I–VI

30 Ten-Minute Plays from the Actors Theatre of Louisville for 2 Actors

30 Ten-Minute Plays from the Actors Theatre of Louisville for 3 Actors

30 Ten-Minute Plays from the Actors Theatre of Louisville for 4, 5, and 6 Actors

2004
THE BEST 10-MINUTE PLAYS
FOR THREE OR MORE ACTORS

Edited by Michael Bigelow Dixon
and Liz Engelman

CONTEMPORARY PLAYWRIGHT SERIES

A Smith and Kraus Book

A Smith and Kraus Book
Published by Smith and Kraus, Inc.
177 Lyme Road, Hanover, NH 03755
www.SmithKraus.com

First Edition: December 2004
10 9 8 7 6 5 4 3 2 1

Manufactured in the United States of America
Cover and Text Design by Julia Hill Gignoux, Freedom Hill Design

ISBN 1-57525-337-2
ISSN: 1550-6746

Contents

Introduction

As we embark on the great adventure of the twenty-first century, the fourth dimension plays a greater and greater role in our lives. The fourth dimension, of course, is time, and in the past century it's been completely redefined. Thanks to Einstein, for instance, we know that time is not a constant but exists only in relation to place and motion. Thanks to Frederick Taylor, time/motion studies have revolutionized the ways we work and play. And thanks to computer scientists, the nanosecond (a billionth of a second!) is now a meaningful measure.

Our hyper-awareness of time has served primarily to accelerate life in every aspect. There's speed-dating and Minute Rice, for example, and that's just the beginning of our postmodern efficiencies. All around us the culture is pushing for greater speed, which requires more energy, which results in more force, which creates more pressure, which causes more stress. While these are difficult factors for most human beings to handle, they provide terrific circumstances for a focused dramatic literature that hopes to reflect life as it's lived — in the fast lane — whether we want it to be or not.

That's why the ten-minute play speaks so directly and metaphorically to our times — no matter where we live. Take these plays, for example. They come from theaters across America and beyond: City Theater in Florida, Chicago Dramatists Workshop, Guthrie Theater in Minneapolis, Actors Theatre of Louisville, Triangle Theater in New York City, A Travelling Jewish Theater in San Francisco, Cincinnati Shakespeare Festival, and Newtown Theatre in Sydney, Australia — to name just a few! The ten-minute play is clearly an international phenomenon — but brevity is not the sole reason for its popularity.

Using the terms of physics, theater consists exclusively of time, space, action and reaction — and by controlling the first of these, we unleash possibilities in the others. Exploring unlimited possibilities within the limits of time, however, demands a writer's creativity. Bingo! That's precisely why the form is so attractive to writers at every level of the profession — because it demands they employ the full powers of their imaginations. And when they tap into that power, the theatrical rewards are incredible. Imagine for a moment how much theatrical magic and thematic resonance could be contained in ten minutes. Now write that play. Or read these plays and perform them for others. It's definitely worth your time.

Michael Bigelow Dixon and Liz Engelman

PLAYS FOR
THREE ACTORS

Aimée

ERIN BLACKWELL

For Nicole

Aimée received a staged reading as part of Playground's Monday Night
Playlab at A Travelling Jewish Theatre, San Francisco, in February 2003.
Amy Mueller directed Danielle Thys (Aimée), Bonnie Akimoto (Madge),
and Brian Herndon (Larry).

CHARACTERS

MADGE, blood-red skirt suit, sprayed hairdo, makeup, deadpan.
AIMÉE, glasses, dyed black hair, black jeans, turtleneck, serene.
LARRY, short-sleeve shirt, tie, tie-pin, buzz cut, earnest.

AIMÉE

Aimée's apartment. Chair overturned. Madge calmly checks her nail polish and condition of her heels. Key in front door, door opens, Aimée enters.

AIMÉE: How did you get in here?

MADGE: Just a routine check.

AIMÉE: Who are you?

MADGE: (*Smiling.*) I'm with Heartland Security. Making you safer.

AIMÉE: What are you doing in my apartment?

MADGE: We'd prefer you didn't raise your voice.

AIMÉE: Answer my question.

MADGE: We'll ask the questions (*Checks paper.*), Miss La Touche. If you'll take a seat, an agent will be with you momentarily.

AIMÉE: You don't understand. I've got to shower, do my hair, fix a bite to eat, and be out of here in ten minutes. If you'd phoned ahead, I would've made time for you. Now, if you'll excuse me, I've got to get into that bathroom.

MADGE: He shouldn't be much longer.

AIMÉE: This is my house.

MADGE: This is United States territory. As such, it constitutes the eminent domain of the United States government. Even if it didn't, we'd find some way around local regulations.

AIMÉE: You can't just walk in here and spoil my evening.

MADGE: Let me remind you, you're on camera. Any resulting video will be edited by our personnel to make you look very, very bad.

AIMÉE: Can I at least make a phone call?

MADGE: If you keep it short and unobjectionable.

(Aimée speed-dials.)

AIMÉE: (*To phone.*) Pick up. Pick up darling. (*Listens to machine, then leaves message.*) Craig. This is not a joke. Heartland Security is here terrorizing me. Help.

(Madge takes phone away with expert skill.)

MADGE: Let's not overdramatize the situation. As soon as we've got what we're looking for, we might leave you alone.

AIMÉE: What if I don't have what you're looking for?

MADGE: Then it could take longer.

AIMÉE: Why don't you just tell me what it is you want? Instead of barging in here like barbarians and — and — dicking around with my personal belongings.

MADGE: *Scientia es potentia.*

AIMÉE: Knowledge is power. Don't start. I've got a Ph.D. in Classics.

MADGE: Then maybe you've forgotten: ignorance is bliss. The less you know about our activities, the happier you'll be.

AIMÉE: My boyfriend has tickets to hear Michael Tilson conduct the San Francisco Symphony in Mahler's Third. Do you know how hard it is to get seats? Do you have any idea how fabulous M.T.T. is with Mahler? Do you realize fin-de-siècle Vienna is not unlike fin-de-siècle California? Mahler's quixotic mood changes, his multicultural layering, his sense of doom and ultimate transfiguration speak to us today in ways too profound . . .

MADGE: I haven't the slightest idea what you're talking about. But isn't it a bit unseemly to rave about a Jewish composer from a decadent empire to a total stranger? Even if I am your friend. Why can't you stay home and watch TV like an American?

AIMÉE: I am an American.

MADGE: We'll be the judge of that.

(Enter Larry, in latex gloves and paper mask, holding plastic bag.)

LARRY: (*Unintelligible.*) I found 'em.

MADGE: Larry, the mask.

LARRY: (*Removes mask.*) Is this the perp?

AIMÉE: Perp?

MADGE: This is Miss La Touche, yes.

AIMÉE: Who are you people?

MADGE: I'm Madge. This is Larry.

(They shake hands amiably and come out fighting.)

LARRY: I'm afraid it doesn't look good. The behavior is chronic, stretching back into adolescence.

AIMÉE: What are you talking about?

LARRY: (*Removes papers from bag.*) Perhaps this will refresh your memory.

AIMÉE: My love letters. You can't touch those.

LARRY: I can and must. For your protection as well as society's. Evil is a canker that eats us from the inside out, Miss La Touche. As I'm sure you'll agree.

AIMÉE: What are you talking about? Is he mad?

MADGE: One of the department's coolest heads.

LARRY: I admit, we've caught this a bit late. If we can't save you, we can stop your infecting others. As compassionate guardians of the nation's moral welfare, it's incumbent upon us —

MADGE: Plain English, Larry.

LARRY: These letters. You admit they're addressed to you. Your name's Amy?

AIMÉE: Aimée.

LARRY: Emmy? Like the award?

AIMÉE: Aimée. French for "beloved."

LARRY: This is more serious than I thought. You recognize this paper?

AIMÉE: Of course. And the handwriting. These are from Paul, my husband.

LARRY: There are other, more recent letters. In a different handwriting.

AIMÉE: Those are from Craig, my boyfriend.

LARRY: Just how many men are we talking about here?

AIMÉE: My husband died five years ago of a rare bone disease. I thought I'd never love again. Then I met Craig. Online. We made a date for a latté. And we've never looked back.

LARRY: I'm going to ask you to read a sentence or two out loud.

AIMÉE: Since when is it a crime to exchange love letters?

MADGE: The personal is the political.

LARRY: *(To Madge.)* See all the French words? *Ambience. Tête-à-tête. Ennui. Je ne sais quoi. Raison d'être. RSVP.* Get a load of this. "This is *l'amour,* Baby. *Le grand amour." (To Aimée.)* You admit having received this letter and shared in its sentiments?

MADGE: Tell the truth. It goes faster.

AIMÉE: Love! What's wrong with love! Don't tell me you pinheads are trying to stop people loving each other?

LARRY: If he meant "love," why didn't he say "love"?

AIMÉE: That's what *l'amour* means, you bonehead.

MADGE: A cooperative attitude now could help you during the sentencing phase.

LARRY: It's a French word, isn't it? *L'amour.* My work in the field suggests love was invented by the French. France has saddled us with a disease that turns men into puppies and women into wolverines.

AIMÉE: Love is the highest value of Western Civilization.

LARRY: Of what?

AIMÉE: Western Civilization.

LARRY: This is America. We do things differently here. You've got a perverse attachment to the decadent penchants of Old Europe, young lady. I'm tempted to classify her an enemy combatant.

AIMÉE: For being in love?

LARRY: For trusting your instincts. For apprehending beauty in the world — in the beloved — without commercial interference or corporate branding. If everyone fell in love — if all 250 million Americans suddenly fell head-over-heels — and started mooning and swooning and pining and whining — sitting in cafés all day, seeking words to express this inexpressable longing in their hearts and loins — and took the trouble to write it out in longhand — with squiggly little birds 'n' bees in the margins — do you know what would happen to the Department of Heartland Security? Have you taken a moment to consider the impact of such self-important behavior on the official watchdogs of your heart?

MADGE: Where are you going with this, Larry?

LARRY: We'd be out of a job. People who love each other don't need us to protect them. Unless we can guarantee a minimum of mistrust and panic, we won't be allowed to run this country.

AIMÉE: You're hallucinating.

LARRY: Am I?

AIMÉE: You exaggerate the destabilizing impact of romance on the body politic.

LARRY: Do I?

AIMÉE: Love's good for the economy. Romance inspires people to eat out. Order in. Go to the movies. Not take down the state.

LARRY: That's not what the handbook says.

AIMÉE: If you'd ever been in love, you'd know how expensive it can get.

LARRY: Just because I control myself doesn't mean I don't feel things. *Au contraire*. I have to practice abstinence, self-discipline, and denial to keep it from all hanging out.

MADGE: Larry?

LARRY: Imagine having to embody the most Puritanical standards of impulse suppression, day after day, while working shoulder-to-shoulder with this fascinating creature.

MADGE: Larry!

LARRY: If I find out I've been going through all this torture for nothing.

MADGE: Larry.

LARRY: If *l'amour* isn't just for Frenchies. If red-blooded Yanks can go googly-eyed. Madge, if it doesn't pose a threat to our nation's security, I've got a time-share up in Mendecino.

MADGE: Maybe we should take this outside.

LARRY: I don't know what's come over me. I feel giddy.

MADGE: Poor thing. Boiling away inside. Why, I don't know whether to report you or . . .

(Aimée guides them to sofa and retrieves her letters.)

AIMÉE: Yes, do that other thing. Use my sofa. You won't be needing my letters.

LARRY: Oh Madge, do you think you could ever like me? Even a little?

MADGE: Larry, you dufus, I'm mad about you.

AIMÉE: (*On her way out.*) *L'amour. L'amour. Toujours l'amour.*

MADGE: Hope you make it to your concert on time.

LARRY: That's what government vehicles are for.

AIMÉE: Oh, no. I couldn't possibly.

LARRY: I insist. Aimée. As a labor of love.

MADGE: After the snooping we've done, I'd feel better being properly introduced to your boyfriend.

LARRY: Craig. What a guy. "This is *l'amour,* Baby." I can learn from him.

(They exit.)

END OF PLAY

The Roads
That Lead Here

LEE BLESSING

The Roads That Lead Here was commissioned by and premiered at
The Guthrie Theater, Joe Dowling, Artistic Director.

CHARACTERS

    JASON, 29, oldest.

    MARCUS, 23, middle.

    XANDER, 20, youngest.

SETTING

    Their father's house.

TIME

    Here and now.

THE ROADS
THAT LEAD HERE

It's bright and warm, the middle of the day. Marcus and Xander sit on a terrace, in white iron lawn chairs. They're huddled over a matching round table which is covered with folders, photos, notepads and various loose scraps of paper. Their speech is rapid, excited, a hint conspiratorial. They are both listening and not listening to each other as they rush excitedly on in their eagerness to share.

MARCUS: *(Thrusting a photo at Xander).* Look at this —

XANDER: Oh, *fantastic!* What is it?

MARCUS: Wolf Point, Montana.

XANDER: I *loved* Wolf Point! I was there last August — no, June. So cold; it actually snowed! *(Of the photo again).* What *is* this?

MARCUS: Grass.

XANDER: *Grass!* It's so yellow.

MARCUS: *Dried* grass.

XANDER: Absolutely. *Dried.* That is so, it's just so . . . it's —

MARCUS: Wolf Point.

XANDER: *Exactly! (Thrusting a photo at Marcus).* Look at *this.*

MARCUS: Great! What is that? Ice?

XANDER: Looks like ice, but it's water. Wave, close up. Pensacola. The sun was glinting —

MARCUS: I see! Spectacular! Jason'll love this. Where is Jason? Why isn't he out here?

XANDER: He's talking to the Eminent.

MARCUS: Still? He's *missing* all this!

XANDER: He'll catch up. We've got all night.

MARCUS: But there's so much. We haven't even seen his yet.

XANDER: Listen to this: *(Picking up a notebook and reading.)* "The dawn sky dipped down in red and white streaks over the endlessly repeating, cream-colored mounds of the empty badlands of west Texas —"

MARCUS: I know! I know!

XANDER: "Interstate 10 pulled me along, a parent tugging a child toward the bright front door of life, no promises, only an endless possibility."

MARCUS: *(Grabbing for a notebook of his own and reading.)* "The earth sinks, as if it were an enormous dish, as I approach Jamestown. Rolling over the far edge, I'm back on the endless table that is the rest of North Dakota —"

(Xander turns to another section of his notebook and starts reading again. Marcus does the same. Both men read simultaneously with furious enthusiasm, almost as though they are "jamming.")

XANDER: "The Columbia River gorge is the one cathedral not built by man. Its very existence is an act of praise. The Oregon side is pure emotion, green and steaming with life. The Washington side is hot, dry, blank — a desert staring at a jungle. Rivers and streams flow down from Mt. Hood like open hands"—

MARCUS: "You could see the whole battlefield from Lookout Mountain. Along the ridge line to the south the monuments stood peeping out silently from under heavy summer trees. They whisper of long-dead regiments from Virginia, Ohio, Minnesota, Tennessee — men who lie here now part of the ridge itself, part of the mountain"—

MARCUS: God, these are so *good*!

XANDER: I've got tons more!

MARCUS: Me, too!

XANDER: Where's *Jason*!? *(Starting to call out.)* Hey, Jace —!

MARCUS: *(Quickly shushing him.)* Don't! You know how the Eminent gets.

XANDER: But there's so much to go over. He's gotta see this. We should meet more than once a year.

MARCUS: No, once is best. We're more independent.

XANDER: Yeah, but if he misses stuff —

MARCUS: Calm down. It'll be fine. We all have to talk with the Eminent.

XANDER: Hey, listen!

(Xander produces a small cassette tape player and plays it: urban noises — traffic, horns honking, skate boarders, a bus going by, dog barks, etc. Marcus listens intently under Xander's stare.)

MARCUS: Denver?

XANDER: Nope.

MARCUS: Denver suburb — Aurora?

XANDER: I wasn't even in Denver this year.

MARCUS: Oh — *Phoenix*!

XANDER: You *bastard*!

MARCUS: *(Laughing at this small victory.)* Try this. *(Marcus produces his own cassette tape player and plays it: ocean surf, gulls screaming, wind, etc.)* Well?

XANDER: Shit. Shit. Lemme listen, lemme . . . um . . .

MARCUS: You have no hope.

XANDER: No, I'm close. It's . . . it's, um . . .

MARCUS: Time!

XANDER: Bethany Beach! Delaware coast!

MARCUS: *Bastard!!*

XANDER: Jace!

    (*Jason has appeared. Unlike his brothers, he seems subdued.*)

MARCUS: How'd it go?

XANDER: Yeah, how's the Eminent?

JASON: He had a present for me.

MARCUS: (*Surprised.*) A present?

JASON: He said since I'm turning thirty this year —

XANDER: Not for two more months —

JASON: And I won't be home for it —

MARCUS: Home? He knows we have to drive.

JASON: That he's going to give it to me now.

XANDER: What is it?

JASON: He wouldn't say. He had a look in his eye, though. I didn't like the look in his eye. (*To Marcus.*) He wants to see you next.

MARCUS: (*Starting to rise.*) Right now?

JASON: (*Shaking his head.*) He'll send word.

    (*A silence hangs over them as Jason sits down with them at the table.*)

XANDER: (*With renewed enthusiasm, trying to banish the uneasiness in the air.*) What'd you bring us, Jace? What've you got?

    (*Distracted, Jason pulls a small piece of darkish fur from his coat pocket. The others stare at it. Xander feels it.*)

XANDER: Wow! Feel this!

MARCUS: What is that? No, wait — make us guess!

    (*They ponder it carefully while Jason stares off in the direction from which he entered.*)

MARCUS: (*Stroking the mystery fur.*) It's not bear; it's too fine.

JASON: There was something different about him this year.

XANDER: Who?

JASON: The Eminent. Something's changed.

MARCUS: Of course things have changed. It's been a year. Things change every time. Wolf?

JASON: No. This was different. There's a look in his eye.

XANDER: Wolverine?

JASON: No.

MARCUS: Otter?

JASON: *(Absently.)* What kind?

MARCUS: Fresh water?

JASON: No.

XANDER: Salt water?

JASON: No.

MARCUS: Bastard! Beaver?

JASON: Getting colder. He said "thirty" in the strangest way. "You're going to be thirty, Jace. You deserve something very special this year." I said my life was already special — that all our lives were special. I mean, what other father would help make a project like ours possible?

MARCUS: Nobody.

XANDER: Dad is very special. Melanistic mountain lion?

JASON: *(At the absurd guess.)* Please. *(Returning to his subject.)* I said Mom would have been proud of him. So few fathers really listen to their sons. So few brothers stay intimately involved in each other's life through adulthood.

MARCUS: It's not raccoon . . . martin?

JASON: No.

MARCUS: Coatamundi? Were you in the Southwest?

JASON: I was all over, like always. No, not coatamundi. *(With a sigh.)* He didn't want to look at my pictures this year.

(The other two look up, shocked.)

XANDER: He *what?*

JASON: Said he expected they looked a lot like last year's.

MARCUS: They're different! There's always something different!

XANDER: This is a compendium! Encyclopedic!

JASON: I know. The whole point is accumulation —

MARCUS: From three different points of view. The gathering of experience.

XANDER: America as we see it.

MARCUS: With fresh eyes. Unjudged. The natural state.

XANDER: Images, writings, smells, tastes — *(Brandishing the fur.)* Feels!

JASON: The Eminent says we're not growing up.

(The others are dumbfounded.)

MARCUS: *We're* not growing up —?! *We're* not!!?

XANDER: How's he spend his day? How's he spend his . . . his . . . majorly grown-up day?! Screwing the public?!

MARCUS: Quiet! He'll hear you!

XANDER: I don't care! How can he say we're not grown up, just 'cause we don't want to go into the business?

JASON: Xander —

XANDER: He spends every waking minute advising mega-corporations how to get around federal law —

JASON: He helps business flow. He's like . . . like a plumber of money.

XANDER: *(Loudly.) Up to his elbows in shit!*

(They all look toward where Jason entered. An anxious moment, but no sound is heard.)

JASON: He was better when Mom was alive.

MARCUS: She always calmed him down.

XANDER: She never even blinked at our gasoline bills.

(They fall into a reverie.)

JASON: You think he got mad that we left again right after the funeral?

MARCUS: That was two years ago!

XANDER: We had to get back on the road.

JASON: I know, I know. Still . . . *(After another silence, as Marcus strokes the fur.)* Fisher.

MARCUS: What?

JASON: The fur. It's fisher.

MARCUS AND XANDER: *(With delight.)* Fisher! You *bastard*!!

XANDER: Great going.

MARCUS: Wonderful animal.

XANDER: Underrated.

(They all ponder the fur.)

JASON: Do you ever wonder if we shouldn't be doing more with our lives?

MARCUS: *More?*

XANDER: How could we be doing more? I drive 200,000 miles a year.

MARCUS: We all do. We have a project. We have a vision.

XANDER: America without the people.

MARCUS: How it survives, despite everything.

JASON: It's just that the Eminent said —

XANDER: Screw the Eminent. Hey, look! I've got some birds' eggs. *(Quickly producing them.)* Quick — Maine or California?

JASON: Xand —

XANDER: Maine or California?

MARCUS: Maine.

XANDER: Nope.

JASON: Guys —

MARCUS: California?

XANDER: Nope! I lied!

MARCUS: No fair!

JASON: *Quiet!! Both of you!!*

    (As they look up, startled at his vehemence.)

JASON: The Eminent — *Dad* — said that he doesn't think our project is . . . helping us grow. *(Over their audible reactions.)* He thinks we should get married, for one thing —

MARCUS: Married? There's plenty of time for that!

XANDER: This is a calling!

MARCUS: These are our years before the mast!

XANDER: Our walkabout!

JASON: We're virgins.

MARCUS: And proud of it!

XANDER: Yeah!

MARCUS: How else are we going to have enough love for this country? It's immense!

XANDER: There's so *much* of it.

JASON: He wants grandkids.

MARCUS: I don't care! Women weaken resolve. When I wake up each morning, I give myself to that first look of the highway — the shadows of the trees crossing the asphalt like ties on a railroad —

XANDER: Or the sun holding the plains in his arms like a sleepy lover —

JASON: You've never *had* a lover! How would you know?!

MARCUS: You talk like you think he's right.

JASON: I'm not saying that, it's just . . .

MARCUS: Just what?

JASON: I miss him sometimes, when I'm on the road.

XANDER: You miss *him*?

JASON: I miss all of you. Don't you?

    (Marcus and Xander look at each other.)

MARCUS: Sure, but . . . you know.

JASON: What?

MARCUS: America is a jealous mistress, Jace.

XANDER: Jealous.

MARCUS: We get lonely — lonely as hell. But when this project is finished, we'll have it all. You know? The whole country. A little touch of everything: pictures, words, plants, animals, objects, textures, soils, water from rivers, oceans, stones, feathers, fur, teeth, claws, thorns, seeds . . .

XANDER: Everything but the people. Everything they don't see, or feel or hear or smell or taste. Everything they forget about, every day — when they're only thinking about themselves or other people. We'll have something for every sense.

MARCUS: Something that *makes* sense.

XANDER: A record of love. A careful record of how much we love America.

MARCUS: Proof that it's still worthy of love. That no matter how many of us there are, no matter how badly we may behave, it's still here.

XANDER: Beautiful. Worthy. Waiting.

(*Marcus puts his hand straight out, palm down. Xander puts his hand on Marcus's. They look at Jason, who pauses. Finally he puts his hand on top of theirs. As they all smile quietly, a DEAFENING EXPLOSION offstage. They stand stunned for a moment, then all rush downstage and look down into the audience as if over a balcony. They're shocked at what they see.*)

JASON: Oh, my God —!!

MARCUS: Jace — it's your car!

XANDER: It's the Eminent!!

MARCUS: He blew it up! He torched your car!

JASON: Oh, my *God*!!!

XANDER: (*To Marcus.*) Hey —! He's going for yours!

MARCUS: Dad —!! *Dad* —! *DAD* —!!

(*Another EXPLOSION. The light of reflected flames dances across their faces. They stare dumbfounded for a long moment. A third EXPLOSION.*)

XANDER: Mine too?

JASON: He bought 'em . . .

MARCUS: And he blew 'em up.

XANDER: I had stuff in my car. From the project.

MARCUS: Me too.

JASON: Me too.

(*Another moment passes as they stare.*)

MARCUS: What's that sign he's holding up?

JASON: I can't read it. All the smoke —

XANDER: (*Struggling to make out the writing.*) It says . . . "You're grounded."

(*All three stare open-mouthed at the burning cars. The reflections of the flames very slowly become the only light. Then there is no light at all.*)

END OF PLAY

Three Dimensions

JEROME HAIRSTON

Three Dimensions was commissioned by and
premiered at the Guthrie Theater,
Joe Dowling, Artistic Director.

THREE DIMENSIONS

Two men stand before a sofa. The sofa faces away from the audience.

A woman sits in a chair away from the men. She occupies a distinctively separate space. She faces towards the audience.

One man studies the face of a digital watch. He pinches it in his hand, fiddling with the buttons.

The other man studies a small stack of photographs, systematically flipping through.

The woman sits silently in her chair, unaffected by the men's exchange . . .

The digital watch beeps. It beeps again.

Art, the one with the watch, flicks the digitized face in frustration.

ART: Dammit. *(Art returns to punching buttons. The watch beeps again. Then again. A long sustained beep. Then again. Under his breath.)* Son of a bitch. *(Squints.)* Fucking small ass buttons.
(Again, a sporadic barrage of beeps. Dale, the one with the photos, looks up.)
DALE: Jesus.
ART: What?
DALE: Enough. I mean, c'mon. Jesus.
ART: Jesus what? What's your —
DALE: *(Re: the couch.)* You'll wake her.
ART: Wake her? *(Art remains focused on the watch, which keeps beeping.)*
DALE: With that. Yes. With that incessant *barrage* of . . . you're bound to . . .
ART: She asked, Dale. You were there.
DALE: We really should just let her —
ART: She was specific. Very specific. No more than an hour. You heard her. You were there.
DALE: It's been days, Art. Days. Not a wink and here she finally . . .

ART: I assured her.

DALE: . . . finally gives in. Finally concedes defeat and you . . .

ART: I *assured* her. One hour and no later. I set this alarm not only so she can rest. But rest assured. And I keep my word, Dale. I do. She knows this. Her whole life she's known this.

DALE: If you say so.

ART: Well, I do. I do. And she does. She knows. So you can kindly —

DALE: Kindly what?

(Sheila, the one who sits alone, adjusts herself in her chair, perhaps re-crosses her legs. The motion prompts Art and Dale to look tentatively to the couch.)

DALE: *(To the sofa, soft.)* Sweety?

ART: Shit, did we . . .

DALE: Sweety? Sweety, are you . . .

ART: Is she?

(Dale studies the couch closer, shakes his head.)

DALE: No. Still gone.

ART: You sure?

DALE: Yeah.

ART: Good. That's good. *(Art faithfully returns to the watch. Another beep.)*

DALE: Christ on a crutch.

ART: That's it. It's done. Alarm's set. All done.

DALE: Unbelievable.

ART: She's now officially . . . *(He holds down a button. One last beep.)* Set. *(Art loops the watch back onto his wrist. Dale returns to the photos. He begins to choose select snapshots, separating them from the stack. Art notices.)* What's that?

DALE: What?

ART: That. What's . . .

DALE: Memorial Day weekend. Blue Ridge.

ART: No, what's that you're doing?

DALE: I don't know. Taking precautions, I guess.

ART: Against?

DALE: Might be a bit much for her, that's all.

ART: Much?

DALE: Seeing herself. Like this. These were just taken.

ART: Yeah?

DALE: It's barely been a week.

ART: And?

DALE: I just don't think it's something to be reminded of. To see herself. Her face. How she used to . . . I don't know.

ART: She's not dead, Dale. There's no "used to." She's still —

DALE: Guess I'd rather save her . . .

ART: She —

DALE: . . . save her the, well, the heartbreak.

ART: She survived.

DALE: *(Pause.)* Yes. Yes she did.

(Pause. Dale returns to sifting photos.)

ART: Give them here.

DALE: I'm not finished.

ART: You're not doing this.

(Dale remains focused on the photos.)

DALE: Correction. Not Blue Ridge. Not all the way Blue Ridge, at least.

ART: I'm serious, Dale.

DALE: Seems there's a St. John or two mingling in here as well.

ART: You're not gonna shame her, OK? Shame her into thinking . . .

DALE: Would you look at her. My God. And that sun.

ART: Thinking she's damaged goods.

DALE: The sky down there.

ART: Thinking she's weak.

DALE: I almost forgot.

ART: When the time came. She opened her eyes. She opened them, Dale. Or did you forget that, too.

DALE: No. I remember.

ART: And I refuse, hear me? I refuse to let you rob her of that. After what she's been through, Hell no. She deserves more.

DALE: Yes she does.

ART: You of all people should know that. What she needs. What she deserves. You of all people.

DALE: Me.

ART: Yes. You. Who saw. Who was by her side. In that room. When she made the choice.

DALE: Choice?

ART: To live through that shit. You know, fight. To open her Goddamn eyes and . . . Like I said, Dale, you should know better. Then to sell her short. You've got no excuse. You were there.

DALE: I was. I was there. *(Pause.)* And you weren't.

ART: What? What did you just say to me?

DALE: I'm just agreeing with you, Arthur. Stating it for the record. I was there. And you. You were not. *(Pause.)* You were never there. For her. Ever.
(Art and Dale look at one another. Silence. Art's watch suddenly begins to wail, the alarm beeping relentlessly.)

ART: Shit. *(Art, panicked, fumbles to stop it. Finally he does.)*
(Art and Dale look to the sofa. After a few moments, their nervous anticipation subsides. They share a silent moment of relief. Art takes off his watch. He holds it in his hand, shaking his head.)

ART: Ridiculous. Fucking ridiculous. I don't know what I'm doing wrong. Here I am. A grown man. And I can't . . . I can't figure this out.

DALE: Art.

ART: Fuck you, Dale. I know what you're thinking. *(Re: the watch.)* Just because I fucked this up, doesn't mean . . . I haven't failed her. Hell, like I need anything to remind me. I know what I'm supposed to do. *(Art moves over to the sofa.)* I'll just stand here and wait. And when it's time, I'll wake her. Just like she wants. Just like she asked. Just like she *trusted* me to do. Now you may not have heard that. But I did. Make no mistake. I heard her. *(Art looks down at the sofa. Dale watches him. Silence. Dale slowly makes his way over to Art. He stands next to him. Dale offers a reconciliatory hand upon Art's shoulder. Art shrugs it off.)*
(Dale walks away. He returns focus to the photos. He takes the selected snapshots and rips them in two. He then walks to the opposite side of the sofa. And looks down upon it. The two men flank the sofa and watch the woman in question "sleep." Stillness. Sheila straightens herself in her seat, bracing herself to speak . . .)

SHEILA: *(To the audience.)* I don't know what I expected, exactly. It's been such a long time since I've done this. I mean, I've closed my eyes so many times in hopes this would happen. And when it did, I figured one of two things would happen. Either one: I'd relive it. You know, each horrific detail. Or two: The opposite would happen. I'd dream of a time or a place where no such thing ever took place. Either way. I didn't expect this.

Apparently there's no scientific reason. I've seen the evidence, passed all the tests. And believe me, there were many. But there was one in particular. I don't know, maybe it's the name. "CAT" scan. Sounds so much more sanguine than X-RAY or MRI. And when I saw it. My mind in three dimensions, trained experts guaranteeing me the integrity of the landscape. Made me feel perhaps that at least here, within quiet confines of my cranium, things would make sense. But to arrive and find, of all things, all of you. Makes one wonder.

For example, right now, I sleep in the presence of two men. Two men who love me. In very different ways, but equally as deep. And I know this, in my bones, my marrow, my heart, to be true. And they have both come to see me through this. And what's so extraordinary is that they do so, despite. Despite history. Despite themselves. Despite each other. They have come unified by one thing, and one thing only . . . Me. So I won't be alone. Which I am not. I am not alone. Even now, as I sleep. I can feel them. I can feel their eyes. Each with their exclusive gaze of relentless devotion. To which I should be grateful. And I so want to be. Grateful, I mean. Grateful and . . . safe. In the company of these two men. Who love me. But still. When I close my eyes . . .

And sleep.

At long last sleep.

And dream. *(She takes in the audience.)* I dream of strangers.

(Art and Dale continue to watch her sleep. Sheila continues to feel them doing so. Slow fade.)

END OF PLAY

Favorite Lady

Leanna Renee Hieber

Favorite Lady was first presented by the
Cincinnati Shakespeare Festival, Cincinnati, Ohio, in 2003.

CHARACTERS

FRANKIE, art student, 20S.
CYNDI, art student, 20S.
LISA, art student, 20S.

PLACE

An art studio in any metropolitan/campus area.

SETTING

Early evening, modern day.

FAVORITE LADY

Lights up on two collegiate ladies: Frankie and Cyndi, sitting on the floor with large sketchbooks on their laps, sliding a beverage between them.

FRANKIE: Hey, Cyn, juried exhibition next week. What did you enter?

CYNDI: Something I *didn't* do in class. *(Beat.)* You know, Hatchworth can go play with himself. Williams can do the same. "Your work is too freeform: it just reduces to symbols." So I like the French Symbolists. Piss off.

FRANKIE: Good thing we're outta here soon. School really isn't your bag.

CYNDI: Gotta know the rules before you can break them.

FRANKIE: Fair enough. So. What're you hanging?

CYNDI: My "Eve was framed" piece.

FRANKIE: OK, which of the "Eve" series is that?

CYNDI: The one where Eve is testifying. Adam's on the defense. Satan the prosecutor. God the judge and George W., Cheney and Ashcroft sit in the jury box eating apple pie.

FRANKIE: *(Grinning.)* Right, right.

CYNDI: It'll be a smash hit. You?

FRANKIE: Still life.

CYNDI: Yeah right. *(Beat.)* You serious?

FRANKIE: *(Holds the stare for a minute, then chuckles.)* Gotcha. You believed me there for a second. I'm showing my favorite oil; the butterfly with the pin through it.

CYNDI: Nice. One last *(Brushes her fingers beneath her chin in a F-you gesture.)* before graduation.

FRANKIE: Ohhhh, did I tell you Hatchworth totally came on to me the other day in the library?

CYNDI: Of course he did.

FRANKIE: I laughed in his face when he asked if I would pose for him. Him and his nudie fix.

CYNDI: Freakjob. *(Beat.)* Hey. You ever wonder . . . back in the day . . . were nudes like porn?

FRANKIE: No. Aesthetics and composition. "The worship of the female form." Has a BFA done nothing for you?

CYNDI: See, that's what they want you to think. Convenient excuse to keep bodies under lenses. No, here's what I'm talking about. The stiff elite in the 1800s; did men go downstairs to their libraries in the middle of the night, draw the velvet curtain in front of their own personal Venus and do their business? I mean, with no Victorian bondage web-sites —

FRANKIE: Just corsets.

CYNDI: God, undressing alone had to require Ghandi-like patience. So my guess is the gents did just that. Quiet. Under cover of night. Just between them and the lady that couldn't say no.

(Beat. Lisa rushes in, clearly stressed.)

LISA: Guys, I need your help.

CYNDI: Wait, don't tell me, a keg in the trunk and nowhere to go?

LISA: Nice try. Not exactly. *(Excited murmur.)* I took her.

FRANKIE: *(Suspiciously.)* . . . Who . . .

LISA: My favorite girl. She's been cooped up in that room for too long. The bastards keep drooling over her and she can't do anything about it. So I rescued her. She's in the car.

CYNDI: *Who?*

LISA: My girl.

FRANKIE: Did I miss a memo? You turn lesbian? A baby you never told us about?

LISA: No, no, no, no — I'll bring her in, just a sec.

(Vanishes. Frankie and Cyndi look at one another.)

FRANKIE: Now I know we've all conspired to carousing, trespassing and the occasional dangerous liaison, but kidnapping?

CYNDI: Wow. Our collective memoirs will rock.

(Lisa pokes her head in, looks around suspiciously, ducks out again, and reenters with a draped, rectangular object.)

CYNDI: Oh, so you're not in trouble with the law.

(Lisa removes the cloth from the picture to reveal one of Paul Gauguin's reclining nudes.)

CYNDI: Oh. Yes. Yes you are.

FRANKIE: Is that what I think it is? Tell me that's just an incredible replica.

LISA: The real deal.

FRANKIE: You stole a Gauguin.

LISA: Rescued a Gauguin.

FRANKIE: Rescued from what?

LISA: The eyes of the public. I can't *stand* how they look at her. It makes me nauseous.

FRANKIE: Well, it's made you a klepto, at least. What were you thinking?! I mean, you're a docent at the damn museum, you *know* how much that is worth. Don't you?

CYNDI: *(Impressed and horrified.)* How in holy hell did you do it?

LISA: She was down while they were fixing some stuff on the ceiling and messing with the power. I was parked by the loading dock on rear gallery shift. Something seized me, it was as if she was calling to me, and I couldn't say no to her.

FRANKIE: Sure you couldn't. I hear her now. "Hey, dimwit, yeah, over here, fifth naked lady on the right. Feel like committing a crime?" There is a point, Lisa, when personification becomes no longer useful but an illness.

CYNDI: I'm not quite sure I get it. I mean, sure we have a love-hate relationship with Gauguin, but —

LISA: I've been watching for years and I just couldn't handle another second. It's like an epidemic.

CYNDI: *What* is?

LISA: It's like . . . lascivious cataracts grow each time they look at her. It's all I can see anymore. A gawking, lewd disease that penetrates into some . . . subversive territory way beyond "art appreciation." I'm like that guy in the Poe story, driven nuts by each glazed eye and I want to put them all under the floorboards.

FRANKIE: But what are they —

LISA: I mean, did *she* invite them in? Was she given a choice? Did she invite them all to undress her with their eyes?

CYNDI: Dude, hate to break it to ya but she's already naked.

LISA: That's not the point.

FRANKIE: Then what is?

LISA: *(Growing exasperated.)* Look. Look at her. Is she asking for it?
(Frankie and Cyndi look at the painting, baffled.)

FRANKIE: Asking for what? If I was her, I'd ask for someone to move the predatory animal a little farther from my ass.

LISA: Maybe it's a gender thing. Maybe you just don't think to look at her like she's fresh meat; ready for any man or beast to pounce. But that's what I see when they see her. They don't think I'm watching, but I am; the voyeur to their voyeurism. A sick circle. You'll never believe this, but yesterday I caught some dude touching himself while looking at her.

CYNDI: *(Turning to Frankie.)* See?! I told you! Hot damn, I'm a genius. I should write a thesis.

LISA: Told you what?

CYNDI: A theory about paintings and private parts.

LISA: I mean, Jesus, where did he think he was? And what happens after Sunday, when I can't be there to look after her anymore? Listen, guys you gotta help me.

FRANKIE: I've never liked the sound of that. Next time, give us a heads up, like "Guys, I'm gonna be a jackass, cover me," so we can then deny your acquaintance. Three times, if needed.

CYNDI: It's not like we can put it above the sofa. They're gonna know you took it. You probably set off some secret alarm — there's a GPS on that son-of-a-bitch and at this very moment the FBI is listening outside the door. What the hell you plan to do with it?

LISA: I didn't think that far ahead. The adrenaline took over.

FRANKIE: Oh, that'll hold up in court.

CYNDI: Hey, the Twinkie defense worked.

FRANKIE: Lisa, return her before you get caught. Seriously.

LISA: I can't. I can't take her back. That . . . that would be like putting a bird in a cage and plucking out its feathers, one by one, stare by stare.

FRANKIE: *What?* Sorry, Lisa, nice metaphor, but ridiculous. *(Beat.)* It's a beautiful painting. Worth lots of money. We could debate ethics and objectification in a Women's Studies class till the cows come home, but the fact is we graduate Sunday and don't *have* to go to class anymore. You wanna trade one prison for another? I mean, it's not just about jail. We're talking about an irreplaceable treasure, a classic piece of art which you of all people were supposed to keep safe.

LISA: But she wasn't safe there. Not from their eyes.

FRANKIE: Looking is rather the point of art.

LISA: What I'm telling you is that there are two types of looking. *I know* the difference, dammit. You learn when *you're* up there, undraped.

(Long silence.)

CYNDI: *(Slowly, glancing cautiously between Lisa and the painting.)* No . . . hey, I see . . . I mean . . . doesn't she seem a little helpless? Look, I mean, Frankie, doesn't she?

(Beat. Frankie is at a loss.)

FRANKIE: God, Lisa, what—

LISA: Mexico.

FRANKIE: What?

LISA: I'll go to Mexico.

CYNDI: Good enough for Frida, why not? You gonna travel with her?

LISA: Too risky.

FRANKIE: *(Wearily.)* Says the felon.

LISA: Not felon, that sounds so vulgar.

FRANKIE: Well, over a million dollars worth of paint and canvas doesn't count as petty theft. *(Frankie gazes at the painting for a long moment.)* She is lovely, though. *(Sigh.)* Gauguin. OK. OK, so I admit Gauguin really pisses me off. His "natives" were a novelty; living among them, claiming mistresses, then painting their fascinatingly brown skin for all of Europe to ogle. Like a work-study brothel he could write off on his taxes.

LISA: See, there's a reason we're best friends.

FRANKIE: While I often share your point of view, Lisa, I've never agreed with your methods.

CYNDI: *(Staring at the painting.)* At least our lives aren't dull.

FRANKIE: Thank God for small favors.

LISA: *(Staring at the painting.)* We can be more than a show-pony. We can exercise a free will she has been denied. I've learned there is a choice as to who sees you day in and day out; who is watching, judging.

CYNDI: Big Brother always is. Ashcroft.

(Suddenly, sirens are heard.)

CYNDI: See? Right on cue. He listens to our every word.

LISA: Oh god. What do I do?

(Beat.)

CYNDI: Destroy the evidence.

FRANKIE/LISA: Hell no/I couldn't.

CYNDI: *(Measured.) Or . . .* send her back to the drooling wolves.

(The girls stare at the painting.)

LISA: *(To the painting.)* What do *you* want, my friend?

FRANKIE: *(Slowly.)* You know, once you reach a conviction, it *is* hard to pretend you haven't. I mean . . . she is . . . so . . .

CYNDI: Do you see the pleading eyes?

(All three girls nod slowly.)

FRANKIE: Almost a wounded animal.

CYNDI: There's only one thing you do for a wounded animal. *(Pause. Cyndi looks up. Beat.)* Well, there's sprinklers, superb ventilation and a concrete floor. *(Cyndi pulls out a box of matches from her pocket.)*

FRANKIE: Oh, God.

LISA: I didn't think it would come to this . . . so suddenly. *(Pause, staring at the painting.)* But it's for the best, isn't it, my favorite lady?
(The girls each light matches and stare at the painting. Sirens. Blackout.)

END OF PLAY

The Office

KATE HOFFOWER

For Robin, Jeanette, and Jillian

The Office premiered at the Chicago Dramatists
Workshop, Chicago, Illinois.

CHARACTERS
ONE
TWO
THREE

TIME
The present.

THE OFFICE

Lights up as an unassuming customer service representative enters (Three). She is normal-looking, on the bland side. She takes a seat at the upstage center desk and begins to shuffle papers. She does not speak, but works quietly at her desk throughout the play. She is rarely acknowledged by One and Two but observes them carefully. Blackout.

Lights up on One and Two slumped in their chairs and/or sprawled across their desks downstage left and right. Their eyes are filled with infinite vacuity.

ONE: I'm bored.

TWO: Me too.

ONE: I've never been this bored.

TWO: Me neither.

ONE: Never in my entire life.

TWO: Never. Not this bored.

ONE: I'm beyond bored.

TWO: I'm *beyond* beyond bored.

ONE: I'm beyond *being* beyond —

TWO: bored.

ONE: I'm —

TWO: so bored.

ONE: So very, very, very —

TWO: bored.

ONE/TWO: I

ONE/TWO: am

ONE/TWO: so

ONE/TWO: bored.

ONE: *(Stuffing a pencil in her ear.)* What time is it?

TWO: *(Stuffing a pencil in her ear.)* Nine AM.

ONE: *(Stuffing a pencil in her nose.)* What time is it now?

TWO: *(Stuffing a pencil in her nose.)* Nine AM and three seconds.

ONE: *(Stuffing her remaining nasal and aural orifices with pencils.)* Now?

TWO: *(Likewise.)* Nine AM and three of the most boring seconds I have ever experienced in my *life.*

ONE: Never

TWO: ever

ONE: have

TWO: I

ONE: ever

TWO: been

ONE: this

ONE/TWO: BORED!

ONE: If I have pretzels on my desk today, and he comes by and eats them again without asking, I'm going to punch him.

TWO: Tell him that's all you can afford to bring to lunch on the miserable salary he pays you, and if he doesn't keep his hands *off*, you'll have him arrested.

ONE: If he fires me, how much can I collect in unemployment?

TWO: Probably more than you're making now. Hey — have you ever noticed that sometimes when he's standing over your desk talking at you that he sort of reaches down and smoothes the front of his pants . . . *excessively*?

ONE: Yes! But it's more like he's patting himself — trying to calm himself down.

TWO: It seems pretty sick to me.

ONE: Maybe it's just a habit.

TWO: Yeah. Maybe when he was a kid his parents wouldn't let him have a pet. So instead of a dog or a cat—

ONE: He started petting *himself*!

ONE/TWO: Aghhhh!!!!!!

TWO: If only he wasn't looking over my shoulder constantly — if he was just here part-time it wouldn't be so bad.

ONE: Yeah, well, good luck. He already works like two hundred hours a week.

TWO: He'd have to cut down if he had a heart attack.

ONE: Great. I'll sneak up behind him and yell boo.

TWO: No. I'm serious. Think about it. The average person burns about two thousand calories a day. And you have to eat thirty-five hundred calories more than you burn in order to gain a pound. He's fairly sedentary, and he doesn't work out or anything. — And I know he easily eats at least two thousand calories a day already. So if we could just get him to eat a little more and gain what? About fifty pounds? Would that do it?

ONE: I don't know. It would help I guess.

TWO: OK. So how long would it take him to gain that much?

ONE: *(Hesitantly.)* Well, thirty-five hundred calories times fifty pounds is . . .

(She uses her calculator.) a hundred-seventy-five thousand extra calories. If he ate — let's say an extra five hundred calories a day — that's like two extra candy bars — it would take. . . .

TWO: A hundred-seventy-five thousand calories?

ONE: Yeah.

TWO: OK. A hundred-seventy-five thousand calories divided by five-hundred is —

ONE: Three-hundred-and-fifty days.

TWO: Almost a year. But maybe it would take less than fifty pounds if we could add more stress to his life.

ONE: Yeah . . . but how would we get him to eat the extra two candy bars a day in the first place?

TWO: It wouldn't have to be candy bars. I could bring in donuts every once in awhile. You could bring in cookies now and then. — And there's always holiday food!

ONE: But what if it works? What if we kill him and get arrested for murder?

TWO: We couldn't get arrested. We didn't *make* him eat it. Besides, he'll probably just have a mild heart attack and have to cut down his work week. That would be perfect.

ONE: I guess so. *(Changing the subject.)* So whadja watch last night?

TWO: Sunday movie. You?

ONE: I went to bed early.

TWO: You always go to bed early.

ONE: You always go home and watch TV.

TWO: No. Sometimes I go home and watch TV and read *People* magazine and eat ice cream —All at the same time.

(Pause.)

ONE: Jesus! Why are we still *here?*

TWO: I don't know.

ONE: I can remember being twelve years old and having my life completely planned out. I was going to graduate from the Eastman School of Music, sing professionally until I was twenty-six, get married, have two children, and then work part time — *if* I felt like it.

TWO: Yikes!

ONE: Well, *you* can't have dreamt of a career in customer service.

TWO: No.

ONE: No.

(Pause.)

TWO: I was going to be a brain surgeon.

> *(Three laughs. One and Two both turn to look at her. Three quickly returns to work.)*

ONE: A *brain* surgeon?

TWO: Yes! I remember watching cartoons one Saturday morning and seeing this commercial for some doll, and all these little girls in pink dresses were sitting around, very well behaved, brushing its hair, practically melting with sweetness. And the next ad was a bunch of boys skating through a fantasy world of castles and dragons, yelling and screaming and having the time of their lives. And then the very next ad was for that same stupid pink doll! So I told my Mom about it and she said, "That's because girls are supposed to sit at home and have babies, and boys are supposed to go out and have a whole hell of a lot of fun and not worry about anything." So I said, "Well I don't want to sit around and have babies. I want to have fun too." And she said, "Great. Be a brain surgeon."

ONE: She said, "Great, be a brain surgeon"?

TWO: She said, "Great. Be a brain surgeon."

ONE: And?

TWO: And I took her seriously. I went to the library and started researching the brain. But then I started having trouble with math and science. I practically failed high school. And I eventually gave up med school dreams for art. . . . I've done some fantastic pastels of the temporal lobe.

ONE: My Dad called me last night. It really scared me because he never calls, so I figured something must be wrong. I couldn't believe it was him. He said, "Are you OK?" And I said, "I'm fine, why?" And he said, "I just got a feeling that something was wrong and I wanted to call." And suddenly I thought — yes Dad. Something *is* wrong. I want to be a singer. I've dreamt about it my entire life but somehow I've ended up here. I work for seven-fifty an hour. I file, I answer phones, and I photo-copy, eight and a half hours a day, forty-two and a half hours a week, and every minute of every day my soul rots away just a little bit more. I'm twenty-eight years old and I'm dying. I'm already dead. I might as well be. I wanted to say, "Make me seven years old again Daddy. Stand with me on the top of the diving board and hold my hand as I look a million miles down at the long black arrows on the bottom of the pool. Then squeeze my hand and tell me that everything is going to be OK. We're just going to count to three and jump."

> *(Pause.)*

TWO: Take your bra off.

ONE: What!?

TWO: I dare you to take your bra off and wear it outside your clothes.

ONE: No! Why?

TWO: It will be a break from the monotony of our otherwise tedious and meaningless lives.

ONE: No!

TWO: I'll let you have the good stapler.

ONE: No.

TWO: I'll change the fax paper for you from now on.

ONE: *No.*

TWO: I'll teach you how to use Quark.

ONE: No . . . . . .

TWO: Quark Xpress, version three point three one. I'll teach you how to set tabs, create master guides, and kern. You will learn how to make entries into the auxiliary dictionary, how to start a new library, and how to import text from Microsoft Word. I can teach you framing, modifying, and how to establish a baseline grid.

ONE: Will you teach me how to use the horizontal/vertical scale?

TWO: Yes!

ONE: OK, OK. I'll do it. But *you* have to do it too.

TWO: Why?

ONE: Because if you do, I'll agree to the heart attack thing. I'll start my part tomorrow by bringing in two dozen double chocolate donuts.

TWO: His favorite!

ONE: Exactly.

TWO: OK. Deal.

ONE: All right then. On your mark —

TWO: Get set —

ONE: Go!

(*They both take off their bras underneath their shirts and re-hook them on top. There can be some ad-libbing, ouches and laughter. Three watches for a moment then silently joins them. They do not notice her. Three sits back down at her desk and resumes work while One and Two finish.*)

ONE: He's going to be here any minute.

TWO: He probably won't even notice!

ONE: He'll probably take one look and start rubbing himself like crazy.

ONE/TWO: Aggghhhh!!!!!!

(*They laugh again and return to their desks. Pause. They begin looking for something to do.*)

TWO: I am really bored.
ONE: Really, really bored.
TWO: Really
ONE: Really
TWO: *Really*
ONE: Bored.
　　(Lights fade to black.)

END OF PLAY

Swan Lake Calhoun

YEHUDA HYMAN

Swan Lake Calhoun premiered at the Beast Festival,
Triangle Theatre, New York, NY.

SCENE

Winter. A frozen lake in Minnesota.

SWAN LAKE CALHOUN

There is a hole in the ice. Two 20 year olds, Benny and Cig, are sitting on folding chairs on the ice-covered lake They are ice fishing and drinking beer. Cig smokes. There are gunshots and then the sound of a flock of geese flying overhead, honking. The guys look up.

BENNY: Hey, look. Swans!

CIG: Swans? Are you retarded? Those are geese.

BENNY: Geese? Are you sure?

CIG: Sure I'm sure. Honkin'. Shittin' all over everything. I hate those fuckin' birds.

BENNY: I dunno. They looked like swans to me.

CIG: That's the problem with you, Benny. You don't see life the way it is. You really must develop a fatal vision.

BENNY: Can't you look on the bright side for once?

CIG: There is no bright side. Look at us: ice fishin' on a Saturday night — it's tragic.

BENNY: We're not so bad off Cig, at least we got jobs.

CIG: White Castle is not a job, Benny, it's incarceration.

BENNY: Nah, c'mon. It's not that bad. We're gettin' that cappuccino machine next week 'n everything. We're gonna be makin' lattés and stuff. It's gonna be really great.

CIG: In your dreams. (*He drains his can, crunches it and pulls another out of his cooler—offers it to Benny.*) Grain Belt?

BENNY: Yuh, thanks.

(*Cig gives the beer to Benny and takes another one for himself.*)

CIG: The thing is — I could die right now and so what? I mean, it's not like I'd really notice or anything.

BENNY: Yuh, I guess me too. Except —

CIG: Except what?

BENNY: I always wanted to go to Morocco.

CIG: Morocco?

BENNY: Yuh, I'd like to see the Casbah. I read about it — winding streets and stuff with hashish and spies and plush, colorful carpets. I'd like to see that before I die. What about you? Isn't there anything you'd like to see before you die?

CIG: No. I'm ready for the end. Bring it on. *(Suddenly his pole starts to jiggle.)* Whoa! Whoa, whoa. It's a big one. Whoa. Whoa, I said — Whoa!!! *(Cig struggles with the fish. It pulls him up off his chair towards the ice hole.)*

BENNY: Cig, you're gonna fall in!

CIG: *(To the fish.)* Fuck you, Walleye, fuck you!.

BENNY: Let it go!

CIG: I got it! *(He gets pulled and falls into the ice hole.)*

BENNY: Cig!

CIG: Help!

BENNY: Cig!

CIG: I can't swim!

BENNY: Neither can I!

CIG: Shit! I'm dying!

BENNY: *(He runs around in panic.)* Uhm! Uhm! Uhm! *(Then he starts to run off.)*

CIG: Where are you going?

BENNY: 911!

CIG: Don't leave me!

BENNY: *(Runs off screaming.)* Help!!!!!

CIG: *(Treading water — shivering.)* I can't fuckin' believe this, I'm actually gonna die. Please — God — or whatever, I didn't mean it — what I said before. I don't wanna die. Not really. Not yet. I was lying before. There is something I want. God this is so hard to say. Just once. I just once want to know . . . *(He goes down. Comes back up.)* I just once want to know. *(He goes down again. Comes up.)* Could you give me a minute? OK? I just once want to know what it's like to love. To really feel it. What it's all about. That's all I'm askin' for. Just once? *(He goes down. Strange and wonderful music: Tchaikovsky. Lena, half woman/half goose, sails in on roller skates: feathers, wings, the whole bit. She wears a backpack. She circles around the ice hole— kneels down and pulls Cig out. He is unconscious. She holds his head in her arms, then leans down and kisses him. Nothing. She honks loudly. Cig wakes, startled.)*

CIG: Huh?

LENA: *(She has a thick Ukranian accent. She lets go of him and looks away.)* Taking off clothings, please.

CIG: What?

LENA: Taking off clothings, please to put these on. *(She takes clothes out of her backpack.)*

CIG: I can't take my clothes off in front of you.

LENA: And why?

CIG: I don't even know you.

LENA: For goodness sake. I am Swan. You think I am interested? Take off before you freezing to death. *(She honks.)* Now!

(He stands up and pulls off clothes. Lena looks away. Hands him pants, etc. as he gets dressed.)

CIG: Uhm, excuse me?

LENA: Yes?

CIG: How come, you can speak English and everything, if you're a goose.

LENA: *(She hisses at him.)* I am not goose.

CIG: I'm sorry, I just thought . . .

LENA: I am swan. 100 percent. Maybe I travel with gooses, maybe I am even looking like gooses but here, in my heart, I am having swan feelings, swan needs, swan desires. Don't call me goose.

CIG: I won't. I didn't understand. . . .

LENA: Yes, you don't understand nothing, you American boys with your drinking and your cappuccinos. You don't know what is to suffer.

CIG: I'm sorry.

LENA: Never mind. Feel better?

CIG: Yeah. Much.

LENA: Well then, good luck Mister. I go. *(She starts to sail off.)*

CIG: Wait!

LENA: What?

CIG: I don't even know your name.

LENA: Is Lena.

CIG: Lena? That's a pretty name. I'm Cig — Sigmund, really. Do you have a last name?

LENA: I can't remember. When the feathers came, I lost many memories.

CIG: When the feathers came?

LENA: I cannot say more. *(She starts to go off again.)*

CIG: Wait, Lena. *(He runs to her. She stops.)* Please. Don't go. *(He takes her arm.)* Your feathers are really soft.

LENA: Yes. We manufacture natural emollient chemical — like lanolin but swannish. It's one of the pluses.

(He strokes her neck. She starts to preen — then pulls away.)

LENA: No more please.

CIG: And you smell nice too.

LENA: Is lavender. It grows over by Lake of the Isles where I live with goose boys. I rub it on myself every morning to hide the smell. I am so ashamed.

CIG: Lena, don't be ashamed. I — I like you.

LENA: Do you know what it is to live with gooses? I am trying all day to keep clean nest but is impossible. You see me like this but you cannot imagine what I was.

CIG: What were you?

LENA: You will not judge and condemn me?

(Cig shakes head.)

LENA: You swear?

CIG: I swear.

LENA: I was born in Ukraine — Kamyanets-Podolsky. There I am having good life. Well, aside from industrial pollution, corruption and staggering un-employment resulting in massive emotional depressivities. Still, I have family and friends and fine achievable goal to be dental technician — but one day — I am seeing advertisement in newspaper — "We find you rich Americansky husband — No finder's fee." My old baba, she says to me, "No, Lena, do not do this. Is bad — beware." But I am saying, "No, babutchka, I will make much money as mail-order bride and bring you to Minnesota where we will live in big fancy condominium with fully stocked sub-zero refrigerator and many other inessential but luxurious items." I dreamed I would be like fairy princess. Now look at me! *(She honks.)*

CIG: What happened?

LENA: I am not reading fine print of contract. "If applicant not finding rich American husband after twenty days, phttt — you are goose!" Now you know truth — I am goose woman.

CIG: But that contract — that's illegal.

LENA: Yes, but what I do? Go on *Court TV*? Now I must only suffer. Suffer for all eternity, unless . . .

CIG: What?

LENA: Unless someone could . . . would . . . no, is impossible.

CIG: Tell me, Lena, please.

LENA: If a man — will stay with me — in my nest — for one night — one whole night — and accept me as I am — with feathers and loud honkings and other various goose unpleasantries — then, in the morning, the curse will be lifted and I will once more again be — ah, I remember now — instead of Goose Woman I will be Lena Osmonova Odetteskaya, aspiring dental technician.

CIG: So, all I have to do is stay with you until morning and you'll become human again?

LENA: Yes.

CIG: Well, that sounds very do-able.

LENA: Really?!

CIG: Except that I have to be at work by 6 AM — cause we're open for break-fast — at White Castle — we're open on Sunday — doesn't that suck?

LENA: *(Insecure.)* OK, fine, no problem — I didn't think it would . . . *(She starts to leave.)*

CIG: No, you don't understand, I want to stay with you — now — all day — forever . . .

LENA: You do?

CIG: Yeah.

LENA: Really?

CIG: Yes, Lena, I — I —

LENA: What? Don't say it.

CIG: I love you!

LENA: No.

CIG: It's true.

LENA: Cig!

CIG: Lena!

(They run to each other. Except she slips, and falls into the ice hole.)

LENA: Cig, help!

(He reaches in and tries to pull her out.)

CIG: Lena, take my arm!

LENA: It is so terribly cold!

CIG: Lena!

LENA: I'm dying, Cig.

CIG: No, Lena, no!

LENA: Yes, Cig, yes — it was inevitable. Happiness was brief but memorable. Now it is over and I am being sucked into the vortex of nothingness. Ah me!

CIG: I can save you!

LENA: No darling. Save yourself. Live. Live and tell the world how once you loved me. Really loved me with much emotion and lack of embarrass-ment. I'm going now.

CIG: No, it's not fair!

LENA: No, but it's beautifully tragic and that is the point. Live. Love. Dasvedanya.

(She pulls a feather out of herself and gives it to Cig. Then, she disappears into the hole — only one graceful swanlike — er, gooselike — arm visible — and then gone.)

CIG: Lena!!!!!!!! *(Cig reaches down. In despair, he collapses on the ice. Looks up. He gets up. Slowly starts to walk away. Looks back at ice hole — reaches for it. MUSIC: "Everything Must Change" sung by Nina Simone. Cig comes back to the hole. He lights a cigarette and smokes it. He sits on the edge of the hole — his feet invisible in the hole. Benny re-enters with rope, a life vest and flippers.)*

BENNY: Cig, you're alive!

CIG: *(He looks up.)* Love, Benny. For the first time in my life, love.

BENNY: When did this happen?

CIG: While you were gone. She was amazing. *(Cig shows the feather to Benny.)*

BENNY: She liked feathers?

CIG: She was . . . a swan.

BENNY: I'm not getting something.

CIG: All right, she was a goose. But to me she was a swan. Now what?

BENNY: Well — we could — now that you're not dying — we could stay and do more fishing.

CIG: Benny, don't you see what's happened?

BENNY: Well, you seem kind of upset.

CIG: It's Morocco, Benny. I've gone someplace and now there's no turning back.

BENNY: Sure there is.

CIG: No Benny, when you love someone — really love someone with all your heart — you're changed — forever.

BENNY: Well, you do look a little different.

(Cig lifts his feet out of the ice hole. He's now wearing "Swan" roller skates. He gets up. He honks. He starts to skate around — flapping his wings with grace and honking.)

BENNY: Cig, cut it out, you're scarin' me!

CIG: Don't be scared, Benny. It's beautiful.

BENNY: What is?

CIG: It's soft as lanolin, sweet as lavender and it has wings. Tell them, Benny. Tell them all!

BENNY: Tell them what?

CIG: Love, Benny. Love has wings!

(He skates off as the sun comes through.)

END OF PLAY

Classyass

CALEEN SINNETTE JENNINGS

Classyass premiered at the Actors Theatre of Louisville,
Humana Festival of New American Plays, 2002.

BIOGRAPHY

Caleen Sinnette Jennings is professor of theater and director of the theater/music theater program at American University in Washington, D.C. She teaches playwriting, acting, directing, and academic courses in theater. She also directs productions for the mainstage. She is a recipient of the 1999 Kennedy Center Fund for New American Plays Award, and a 2002 Heideman Award from the Actors Theatre of Louisville.

CHARACTERS

AMA, or AMADEUS, black college freshman.
BIGB, or BELINDA, black woman, 20, dressed like a street person.
MILES, white college senior and radio station manager.

SETTING

A small room that serves as a modest campus radio studio at Bellmore College. Ama speaks into the mic with a suave broadcaster's voice.

CLASSYASS

AMA: OK you Bellmore boneheads, that was Tchaikovsky's "1812 Overture." Bet those cannons busted a couple of you dozers. Perfect for 3:47 AM on a cold, rainy Thursday in finals week. It's the end of time at the end of the line. Study on, people. Bang out papers. Cram the facts. Justify that exorbitant tuition and make Bellmore College proud. I'M FEELING Y'ALL! Especially those of you studying for Calc 801 with Professor Cobb. Call me if you have a clue about question # 3 on page 551. You're listening to Casual Classics, because you don't have to be uptight and white to love classical music. This is WBMR, the radio station of Bellmore College. Miles Morgan is your station manager. I'm Ama — Amadeus Waddlington, with you till 6 AM Guzzle that warm Red Bull and cold Maxwell House. Here's music to squeeze your brains by. It's Dvorjak's "New World Symphony" comin' atcha. *(He puts on the CD, grabs a beer and a huge textbook, and sprawls out on the floor. A bold knock interrupts him. He shouts.)* Go to hell, Miles. I like "New World"!
(Another knock.)

AMA: OK, OK. I'll play Beethoven's Symphony #1 next. Lots of strings, OK? *(Persistent knocking.)*

AMA: Damn! *(Ama strides to the door and opens it. BigB strides in, carrying shopping bags and waving several faxes.)*

BIGB: You messed up, boy!

AMA: Excuse me?

BIGB: And your smart-assed faxes made it worse!

AMA: Do I know you?

BIGB: *(Examining the mic and CDs.)* I want a public apology.

AMA: Don't touch that! Listen, whoever you are. . . .

BIGB: Whomever!

AMA: Whatever!

BIGB: You ain't got a clue who I am.

AMA: A fabulous person, no doubt, but you've got to go. This is a classical music show and I've got a killer calculus final tomorrow.

BIGB: Color me compassionate. You're shorter than I thought. But I figured right about you being a dumb ass. I told you right here . . . *(BigB shows Ama the faxes and he realizes who she is.)*

AMA: Oh my God . . . you're . . . BigB! I thought you were . . .

BIGB: . . . a brother, I know, 'cause I ain't hearing none of your bullshit. Well, I thought you was a white boy, and I was right.

AMA: Look, I don't know what you want. . . .

BIGB: How long I been faxing you, moron? You said the "Gloria" was by Faure . . .

AMA: . . . As I told you one thousand faxes ago, "Gloria" is by Poulenc and when I played it, I said Poulenc . . .

BIGB: . . . Faure!

AMA: . . . Poulenc!

BIGB: I know what I heard, you arrogant shithead.

AMA: Does that BigB stand for "bitch" or "borderline psychotic"?

BIGB: I ain't even 'pressed by you trottin' out them tired SAT joints. I'm down at the Palmer Street Shelter, which you knew by the headin' on the fax, and you just figured I didn't know shit about classical music.

AMA: BigB, I'm truly flattered that you even listen, but you don't . . .

BIGB: My crew at the shelter want to come up here and kick yo ass.

AMA: Whoa, whoa there. I'm sorry about our misunderstanding, OK?

BIGB: And that s'posed to float my boat?

AMA: Let's be calm, OK, B?

BIGB: BigB to you, and I know you ain't s'posed to be drink'n beer up in here.

AMA: You never saw that.

BIGB: Now I got two things on ya. This gonna be what they call an interesting evening. *(Thumbing through his calculus book.)* This the shit probably got your brain too messed up to know your Poulenc from your Faure. *(She sips Ama's beer.)*

AMA: Don't do that. Suppose I have a social disease?

BIGB: Ha! Bet you still a cherry.

AMA: Suppose YOU have a social disease?

BIGB: I'll just call your Dean and tell him I caught it sippin' outta your freshman-ass beer bottle.

AMA: What do you want from me?

BIGB: You made me look stupid in front of my crew.

AMA: Look, I'm just a nerd playing dead white men's music. Why do you even listen to my show?

BIGB: So a sister like me ain't s'posed to be a classical music affectionado.

AMA: The word's "afficianado". . . .

BIGB: Boy, I'm feelin better 'n better about bustin' yo ass.

AMA: This is like something out of Scorcese. If I apologize for the thing I DID NOT DO, will you go?

BIGB: Maybe. Or maybe I'll stay and watch you work awhile.

AMA: It's against the rules.

BIGB: Lots of things against the rules, freshman boy. Don't mean they ain't delicious to do.

AMA: If my station manager comes in . . .

BIGB: Tell him I'm studyin' witcha, that we putting the "us" in calculus.

AMA: Well, you don't exactly look like a student.

BIGB: Well, you don't exactly look like a asshole, but you the poster boy. Where you get "Ama" from anyway?

AMA: Wolfgang *Amadeus* Mozart. My dad's a classical musician.

BIGB: Oh yeah? Where he play at?

AMA: He sells insurance. No major symphony'll hire him.

BIGB: I know that's right. Oughta be called "sym-phoney" — like phoney baloney, right?

AMA: *(Patronizingly.)* That's very clever, BigB, but I've got a lot of work to do. How about I give you and your people at the shelter a, what do you call it, a "shout out." Right in the middle of Dvorjak. How would you like that? *(Ama goes to the mic, but BigB stops him.)*

BIGB: How you gonna interrupt "New World Symphony" and mess up everybody's flow? You crazy, Amadeus Waddlington. You also a lucky bastard. BigB like you. She gonna take it easy on you.

AMA: Why does your use of the third person chill my blood?

BIGB: Take me to dinner and we cool.

AMA: What?

BIGB: Over there to the Purple Pheasant, where the President of Bellmore College eat at!

AMA: . . . Are you crazy? I don't have that kind of . . .

BIGB: . . . an' buy me a present . . .

AMA: . . . a present? I'm broke!

BIGB: . . . somethin', how they say it, "droll." Yeah, "droll" and "ironic"! Like a CD of "Dialogues of the Carmelites" by POULENC. I can see you 'n me sittin' up in the Purple Pheasant, chucklin' over our little in-joke, sippin' a half-ass California pinot grigio.

AMA: Who the hell writes your material?

BIGB: And pick me up in a shiny new car.

AMA: Hello? Freshman aren't allowed to have cars.

BIGB: Beg, borrow or steal, my brother, but you better have yo ass waiting for me at the shelter tomorrow night at 7:30. And don't shit in your khaki's. My boys'll watch your back in the 'hood.

AMA: You're delusional.

BIGB: Oh, you insultin' BigB, now? You don't wanna be seen with her?

AMA: I'd love to be seen with her . . . you! I'd give my right arm to have the whole town and the President of Bellmore see me escort you into the Purple Pheasant. Hell, I'd even invite my parents. But I'm a scholarship student with five bucks to my name.

BIGB: *(Sniffing him.)* Ya wearing cashmere and ya reek of Hugo Boss. Don't even try to play me, boy.

AMA: Maxed out credit cards, BigB. I'm just a half-ass wannabe freshman with a little gig, trying to make some headway with Mr. Mastercard. I'll apologize on air. I'll stamp your name on my forehead, I'll run naked down the quad and bark like a dog . . .

BIGB: . . . anything but take me out. You're a snob, Amadeus Waddlington. You a broke-ass, cashmere wearin shit-talkin' loser who don't know his Poulenc from his Faure . . . *(BigB finishes off Ama's beer.)* . . . and drinks lite beer! My crew was right. Ya need a beat down.

AMA: BigB, please . . .

BIGB: See, I be down at the shelter, diggin on ya voice early in the mornin'. People say you ain't shit, but you gotta way a soundin' all mellow an' sexy. And when you spank that Rachmaninoff, oh yeah, baby! So when you screw up the Poulenc I send a friendly fax to point out yo error and help yo ass out. . . .

AMA: And I appreciate. . . .

BIGB: But you had to get up in my grill wit that, "what-do-you-know-about-classical-music-you-stupid ass-homeless-crackhead" kind of attitude. *(She starts to leave.)* Well, Palmer Street crew will be very happy to whup yo behind.

AMA: *(Stopping her.)* I didn't mean to give you attitude. I'm sorry. I'm broke, I swear! I'll show you my bills, I'll show you my bank statements. Isn't there anything else I can do, BigB? Please!

(Pause. BigB looks Ama up and down, to his great discomfort.)

BIGB: Kiss me.

AMA: What did you say?

BIGB: I'm getting' somethin' outta this deal. Kiss me.

AMA: But. . . .

BIGB: Not one them air fly by's, neither. Gimme some tongue!

AMA: Oh God.

BIGB: *(She advances on him.)* Lay it on me, Amadeus Waddlington. Kiss me or kiss yo ass good-bye.

AMA: *(Backing away, near tears.)* This isn't Scorcese, it's John Woo.

BIGB: Come on classyass, pucker up! *(BigB tackles Ama and plants a long, deep, kiss on him. When she lets him go, Ama steps back, looks at her, touches his mouth, and faints. BigB kneels calmly beside him. Her entire demeanor changes. Her voice is rich, cultured, her grammar impeccable. She sits him up and gives him a few light slaps.)* Hey! Hey! Ama? Damn it, Amadeus Waddlington, wake up!

(Miles Morgan enters drinking a beer.)

MILES: Who are you, and what the hell did you do to Waddlington?

BIGB: He just fainted. Get something cold.

(Miles pours cold beer on Ama's head. Ama comes to.)

BIGB: Have you sufficiently recuperated Mr. Waddlington?

MILES: *(To BigB.)* Hey, you look familiar . . . where do I know you from? . . . in the paper. . . . from the shelter. You're . . . Man you sure look. . . . different! Oh my God . . . You're not going to tell your father about the beer, are you? I'm a fifth year senior trying to graduate . . .

BIGB: Just make sure he's OK.

(Miles bends down to Ama who grabs him by the collar. They whisper urgently, while BigB thumbs through the CDs and eavesdrops, greatly amused.)

AMA: Oh God. Oh God! I kissed her!

MILES: Way to go, man!

AMA: I'm gonna die!

MILES: She's that good, huh? Bet she's a knockout under all that stuff she's wearing. You all going to a costume party or something?

AMA: Don't you get it, Miles? I kissed her!

MILES: Lucky bastard! Kickn' it with Dean Stafford's daughter.

AMA: *(After a beat.)* What did you say?

MILES: That's Belinda Stafford, Dean Stafford's youngest daughter! She dropped out of Bellmore to work at the shelter. It was all in the papers and everything.

BELINDA: *(Handing him money.)* Thanks for the beer and the amusement, Mr. Waddlington.

AMA: Is this true? Are you really . . . ?

BELINDA: *(Removing her dirty garments and putting them in a bag.)* I work night shifts at the Palmer Street Shelter. You can imagine that some of the women find it hard to sleep. Your music and your incredibly boring commentary usually do the trick. Everything was fine until you responded so rudely to my fax. You assumed because it came from the shelter . . .

AMA: No . . . I just . . . I didn't . . .

BELINDA: You're an arrogant, ill-informed, elitist, Amadeus Waddlington. I've known guys like you all my life. It broke Daddy's heart when I dropped out of Bellmore, but your faxes reminded me exactly why I did it. So, I decided to teach you a lesson. You're not going to die from my kiss, but I hope you won't forget what it felt like to think that you were. *(She scatters the faxes over his head and starts to exit.)*

MILES: Now, uh, Ms. Stafford, you wouldn't mention this to your father . . .

BELINDA: I've got people without winter coats on my mind.

AMA: *(Rushes to her.)* BigB, I mean Belinda, I mean, Ms. Stafford, please wait. I get a lot of shit from people about this show and I thought you were just another brother hassling me. I don't have an attitude about the shelter because I've got too many poor folks in my own family. I'm sorry about the vibe. Can I make it up to you? Maybe put in some hours at the shelter?

BELINDA: If you think you can hack it. I picked out some CDs for you to play. My people sleep well to Debussy. I'll be checkin' you! *(She puts on her headphones as she exits.)*

MILES: And you won't mention this to. . . .

(Miles exits calling after Belinda. Ama suddenly remembers he's on air. He runs to the mic.)

AMA: Yo, my people, was that dope? Bet the "New World Symphony" woke yo asses up! Hey, I'm still waiting to speak to anybody with a clue to number three on page 551 in Cobb's calculus class. Anybody? It's 3:59 on WBMR the voice of Bellmore College. I'm Amadeus Waddlington and this is Casual Classics, because you don't have be uptight and white to love classical music. You don't have to be a snob either. I wanna give a shout out to my girl BigB. I think I'm in love, people. Yo, B, I apologize. "Gloria" was, is, and always will be Poulenc. I dig the lesson . . . *(He touches his lips.)* and I dig the way you taught it. I'll be down to lend a hand, you better believe that. And for the folks listening at the Palmer Street Shelter, here's a little Debussy to soothe you to sleep. Better times ahead, my people. Better times ahead.

(Lights dim as sounds of Debussy come up. Blackout.)

END OF PLAY

Airborne

GIB JOHNSON

Airborne was first produced by City Theatre for SUMMER SHORTS '98, Coral Gables, Florida, on Thursday, June 4, 1998.

AIRBORNE

A drab conference room at an airport. The faint sound of jets landing and taking off. Outside, announcements are made in various languages. In the room, a table and chairs. On the table are Styrofoam cups, a thick manila folder and pens. Sawyer, a professional woman, sits at table clicking her ball-point pen. A male Doctor, dressed in shirt, corduroy trousers and knit tie, stares out at audience. He seems preoccupied.

SAWYER: I think the thing we have to do now is to get her signature on the forms. That way we can just put it behind us. Just get the signature and wrap things up quickly.

DOCTOR: *(Pause.)* I want to talk to her. I'd like my report to be complete.

SAWYER: Bobby, I've done scores of these situations, and they're all lambs while they still work for the airline, but once they're dismissed and have an attorney working on a percentage, they're monsters. She could come back and say anything. She could say it was stress related. Say her supervisors were harassing her. The airline needs her to sign.

DOCTOR: I need a few more things so the report's complete. I'm sure you don't want anyone second-guessing us later.

SAWYER: Bobby, she can't stay.

DOCTOR: I understand, Sally, but a few minutes won't matter.

SAWYER: Our asses are on the line with "Legal" if she doesn't sign.

DOCTOR: I'd like to talk to her.

SAWYER: Why, Bobby? Why?

DOCTOR: *(Pause.)* Once she's gone . . . we'll never know.

(Sawyer looks exasperated, but in a moment she leaves the room. Doctor goes to thick manila personnel file on desk and flips through it intently, looking for an explanation . . . a key to the puzzle. After a moment, Sawyer leads Lisa Newcombe into the room and closes the door behind her. Lisa is a delicate looking woman dressed in an immaculate airlines ticket agent uniform.)

LISA: Hello, doctor. I didn't know if I was going to see you again.

DOCTOR: Oh, no, Lisa. I wanted to see you again very much. Have a seat. *(Gestures to chair.)* . . . please.
(Lisa takes a seat at the table.)

LISA: I'm glad you got over your cold. It takes me forever to shake them.

DOCTOR: Thanks. My wife made me stay in bed for a few days.

(Lisa seems slightly saddened by this remark.)

LISA: Oh, how wonderful. She looks out for you.

(Sawyer stands in the shadows behind Lisa. Doctor has Lisa's personnel file in hand.)

SAWYER: We were wondering if you'd feel comfortable enough . . .

DOCTOR: Lisa, for the most part, you've got an outstanding record. You've worked for the airline — what? — nine years?

LISA: *(Proudly.)* *Ten* years in December.

DOCTOR: You must have a lot of wonderful friends at the airline by now.

LISA: *(Uncomfortable.)* I do, doctor. I do. I'm blessed. Then, at the end of the day, we all go our separate ways.

DOCTOR: I wonder then if you can tell me the first time you . . . exceeded policy.

LISA: I don't think . . .

DOCTOR: One of the first times then.

(Lisa pauses, reflects for several moments. This is difficult.)

LISA: Three, I mean, no . . . three, maybe four years ago. I was on my PM shift and a heavyset businessman approached me. He was carrying all this luggage, and seemed out of breath. He kind of wheezed when he wasn't talking. He looked so tired — tired of the world, doctor.

DOCTOR: Do you remember his name?

LISA: No, but I remember he asked for low-salt meals. He was bound for business in Tokyo and he wanted low-salt meals. But doctor, he looked so exhausted. I don't know what he was thinking, letting himself get so run down and then getting on a long plane flight. *(Looks to Sawyer.)* Long flights can dehydrate you. *(Looks back to the doctor.)*

DOCTOR: You felt sorry for him.

LISA: I was worried about his health. And so . . . while he stood there, it came to me. This man should be swimming in a blue tropical lagoon, not doing more business in Tokyo. It was my feeling that the Tokyo trip could wait. *(Pause.)* And I remember thinking, "This is crazy, Lisa. What are you doing? You have no business interfering in this man's life." But finally, I just decided he needed someone to look out for him.

DOCTOR: So you . . .

LISA: . . . changed his destination. Shift, keystroke, keystroke, code, enter. And he was on his way to Hawaii, the Big Island. *(Lisa turns to Sawyer.)* The one with the black rock, Ms. Sawyer.

SAWYER: *(Sharply.)* Yes, I know. Thank you.

DOCTOR: He didn't question you about the flight number?

LISA: *(Small laugh.)* Well, doctor, thanks to Ms. Sawyer and all the other fine people in Personnel, I've learned to be very reassuring. People are jittery enough about flying without the equivocation of a ticket agent. I simply told the man that the flight number would change when he arrived in Hawaii.

SAWYER: He didn't question it?

LISA: Oh, yes, yes, he did. But at that point I bumped him up to first class and *(Laughs.)* . . . the tiniest smile crossed his face for the first time. *(Smiles.)* I mean, he had a really lovely, boyish smile. I told him he was the only one in first class going to Tokyo. And then he went to his plane. Except that flight never went to Tokyo and, personally, I'm hoping he found a beautiful blue Hawaiian lagoon to swim in. Maybe one with yellow fish. I like to think of him swimming with yellow fish.

DOCTOR: And what happened at that point?

(A startled expression crosses Lisa's face.)

LISA: Nothing! That's what amazed me! The next day I was sure I'd be fired. I even brought a cardboard box to bring my belongings home. But no one ever said a thing. No one! Not a word.

DOCTOR: And that pleased you?

LISA: He needed someone to take care of him.

DOCTOR: Why do you suppose it started?

LISA: I haven't a clue. Really I don't.

SAWYER: Lisa, I don't want to take any more of your time than necessary. If you'd like, you can sign right now. *(Points to documents.)*

DOCTOR: It happened again, didn't it?

LISA: Uh-huh. A few weeks later, this young family approached my ticket station. The parents were arguing, their baby had a cold, and they were just completely out of sorts. In fact, the mother was snappish with me. I didn't take it personally, though. And that baby, can you imagine having to take that sick baby back to Chicago in the middle of winter? I'm sure it was on that poor mother's mind. And then I thought, if they were in a better frame of mind, they'd be lovely people. Really lovely.

DOCTOR: You did something again.

LISA: Yes. *(Pause.)* I did. Shift, keystroke, keystroke, code, enter. They were on their way to Phoenix. Phoenix is just wonderful in the winter. A guaranteed eighty degrees and you can golf among the saguaro cactus. Plenty of art galleries in Scottsdale, too. I thought the heat would be just right for the baby's cold. *(Closes her eyes.)* I just visualized that child breathing the warm desert air. It just seemed to me they needed a friend. Those of us who are lucky forget what it's like not to have someone around to care for us.

DOCTOR: You ticketed them to Phoenix, but told them it was a layover to Chicago.

(Lisa nods enthusiastically.)

LISA: They never got closer than two thousand miles from Chicago on that trip. Not that Chicago isn't a fine city. *(Pause.)* Gateway to the Midwest and all.

DOCTOR: And the couple accepted your explanation.

(Lisa smiles at Sawyer.)

LISA: Thanks to the fine training I received from Ms. Sawyer and the wonderful people in Personnel.

(Sawyer grimaces.)

LISA: We're taught to inspire confidence.

DOCTOR: And what happened?

LISA: *(Smiles.)* Nothing! Nothing from my superiors, nothing from the family. It just amazed me. They must have had a wonderful time in Phoenix. I hope they played golf. Have you ever been to Phoenix, Ms. Sawyer?

SAWYER: *(Deadpan.)* No. *(Pause.)* I've never vacationed in Phoenix.

LISA: Doctor?

DOCTOR: A college buddy practices tax law there.

LISA: I'd recommend you stay at the Phoenician. They have a fabulous nutritionist. And have dinner at Ruth's Chris Steak House.

DOCTOR: Sounds like you've spent a lot of time there.

LISA: Me? No. I just read guidebooks at the library on my days off. Or else I bring them back to my apartment at night and read them after I feed and comb my cat. She starts clawing my couch if I'm not home on time. So I go home and read the books. Fodor's are good, but I especially like the Michelin.

DOCTOR: Lisa, was there any change in your private life that coincides with this period? Some disappointment?

LISA: Not that I can remember.

DOCTOR: The death of a loved one?

LISA: No.

DOCTOR: The end of a romance?

(Lisa laughs a little too loudly as if this is ridiculous.)

LISA: Not that! God, I'm way too busy having fun and pursuing my interests. I'm just always on the go. After I feed kitty, I'm out the door. Night classes. My work at the animal shelter. *(Pause.)* I guess I just wanted that family to be happy and healthy again. That's all. I think they needed someone. Nothing complicated.

DOCTOR: You altered more and more destinations, didn't you.

LISA: Yes. That's true.

DOCTOR: How many do you expect you changed the first year?

(Lisa thinks.)

LISA: About ten.

(Sawyer grimaces.)

DOCTOR: And the second year?

LISA: Thirty-five . . .

SAWYER: Jesus!

LISA: . . . or forty.

(Sawyer shakes her head in amazement.)

SAWYER: Are you going to explain this? Are you going to explain this or are you just going to sit there and stonewall? Because your whim could've subjected this airline to . . .

DOCTOR: Sally . . .

SAWYER: . . . any number of lawsuits.

DOCTOR: Enough, Sally.

SAWYER: Bobby, what are you talking about?

DOCTOR: Nothing happened.

SAWYER: Well, something could have happened!

LISA: I'm sorry. I am. I know this exceeds company guidelines.

(Sawyer goes to manila file on table, takes two documents and slaps them in front of Lisa.)

SAWYER: Lisa, it's time to sign this termination agreement. It just makes clear the conditions of dismissal. So there's no misunderstanding or unpleasantness later.

(Lisa reaches over to sign.)

DOCTOR: Lisa, you ought to talk to a lawyer first.

SAWYER: I think it would be best if she signed now, Bobby.

(Lisa becomes agitated.)

LISA: Ms. Sawyer . . .

DOCTOR: I'm the doctor here!

LISA: You don't have to get upset on my . . .

SAWYER: You're the *airline's* doctor! We hired you.

(Lisa gets even more agitated.)

LISA: Doctor, please . . .

SAWYER: *(Angrily.)* Bobby, do you want your consulting contract with the airline reviewed? Because you're supposed to be working for us.

DOCTOR: I *answer* to the state medical board!

SAWYER: Well, then, maybe they'd like to pay your salary.

(Lisa suddenly reaches over and quickly signs the documents. Doctor sees this.)

DOCTOR: Lisa!

LISA: There! It's done. It's not worth the two of you getting upset, is it? Two close colleagues. Two friends. It's not worth that. I don't think so. I've always thought that it's important for friends to look out for each other. It'd be a pretty sad world if we didn't have someone to look out for us. *(Lisa pauses for a moment, then looks up and notices Doctor and Sawyer staring at her. Lisa pulls herself together.)* I don't mind signing, Ms. Sawyer. I'm not going to sue the airline. I'm a busy person. I've got so many interests. I've got a very happy and fulfilling life. *(Pause.)* It's kind of like a novel, and I'm looking forward to the next chapter.

(Lisa picks up the signed document and hands it to Sawyer. Sawyer takes the document, puts it in Lisa's employee folder. Lisa starts to slowly leave the room.)

SAWYER: It'd be best if you return your uniforms and other airline property promptly, Lisa. We can avoid more trouble that way. *(Sawyer gives insincere smile. Lisa takes a few more steps.)*

DOCTOR: *(To Sawyer.)* Aren't you going to give her the letter?

SAWYER: Anything you or I do or say . . .

DOCTOR: *(Shouts.)* For chrissake's, Sally, give her the letter!

(Sawyer pauses, opens file, thumbs through pages, finds a letter on small pink stationery and hands it to Lisa. Lisa takes it. As Lisa reads the letter, her expression slowly changes from anxiety to bewilderment to deep contentment. Finally, Lisa looks up at Doctor.)

LISA: That's nice. That's really beautiful. I remember them. They were traveling with her grandmother. *(Pause.)* "Nana." They called her "Nana."

DOCTOR: *(Emotional.)* You changed their lives forever, Lisa. They'll never forget you. Do you understand that? They'll never forget you.

(Pause, then Lisa speaks dreamily to herself.)

LISA: They just needed someone to look after them, doctor. It's not that difficult to understand. We all need someone to look after us. *(Pause. Then Lisa jerks to alertness and looks around at Doctor and Sawyer staring at her.)* Isn't it lucky we all have someone to do that? *(Lisa slowly puts the letter on the conference table and exits. Doctor and Sawyer stare after her.)*

(Blackout.)

END OF PLAY

The Some of All Parts

Mrinalini Kamath

The Some of All Parts premiered at the Newtown Theatre,
Short & Sweet Play Festival, Sydney, Australia.

CHARACTERS

MARGARET, a woman in her mid to late 20s.
JONATHAN, a man in his mid to late 20s.
LESTER, male, pleasure personified.

TIME

The present.

SETTING

A studio apartment.

THE SOME OF ALL PARTS

We hear faint laughter and then the sound of a key in a lock. The door opens and the light comes up on a modestly furnished studio apartment in Manhattan. Margaret and Jonathan, a woman and man in their mid to late 20s enter. They make a rather nice-looking couple.

JONATHAN: So how about the Indian art exhibit on Sunday?

MARGARET: That sounds great.

(Margaret starts to take off her coat — Jonathan helps her with it and hangs it up on the coat stand. He takes off his coat, hangs it up, and when he turns around, Margaret immediately kisses him on the mouth.)

JONATHAN: Oh.

(Margaret kisses him again, and still kissing him, pulls him in the direction of her bed.)

JONATHAN: Uh . . . what . . . where are we going?

MARGARET: I just thought I'd move things along to the bed. *(She tugs him again. He doesn't budge.)* Well, come on.

JONATHAN: You know, I think we should go a bit slower, maybe have some wine —

MARGARET: I don't think I have any. *(She starts to nuzzle him.)*

JONATHAN: *(Stealing a look at his watch.)* If you don't have any, I could just run downstairs and buy a bottle. I think we passed a liquor store on the way here, didn't we? Nothing like wine for getting in the mood . . .

MARGARET: Nah, that's OK, I'm already in the mood, we don't need wine. *(She starts pulling him toward the bed again.)*

JONATHAN: Oh. All right. *(He slowly starts to go with her then comes to an abrupt stop.)* Candles!

MARGARET: What?

JONATHAN: Nothing provides that romantic, sexy ambience like candles.

MARGARET: You want candles.

JONATHAN: *(Fervently.)* I *need* candles.

MARGARET: I'm afraid I don't have any.

JONATHAN: No? Well, how about I go get some?

(Pause.)

MARGARET: Jonathan . . . is something the matter?

JONATHAN: No, nothing's the matter. Why?

MARGARET: Well, you seem to be . . . Is it me? Do you find me . . . ? Because if you do, I don't think it was fair for you to string me along —

JONATHAN: Oh no, not at all. I just . . . I know that most women don't like to rush things, that's all —

MARGARET: If this were our first date, that would make sense. But we're up to date number four, I have invited you up and I want to tell you, I'm OK with going ahead and having sex. In fact, I'm more than OK with it, I'm all for it. *(She shakes an imaginary cheerleading pom-pom.)* Yay, sex! *(She takes him by the hand and tries to move in the direction of the bed again. Jonathan stands still.)* So why don't we —

JONATHAN: I'm sorry, but it just doesn't feel right to rush into things like this. I mean, romance is still alive, right? So why don't I go out and —

MARGARET: Jonathan — I don't want to be indelicate, or anything — but, did your last girlfriend — was she critical of you? Because I think I should tell you, just because one woman doesn't appreciate what you're doing doesn't mean —

JONATHAN: No, no, what gave you that idea?

MARGARET: It's just . . . look, I'm very non-*judgmental,* so if you're worried that you won't be able to live up to my expectations —

JONATHAN: No, no, I'm fine with your expectations. Hell, the bigger they are, the better!

MARGARET: Oh. *(Pause.)* Uh, I think you're going to have to help me here, because this is . . . is my apartment some sort of . . . is it giving you a weird vibe, or something, because I've never encountered anything like this before.

JONATHAN: Anything like what?

MARGARET: Well, you're a man, right? I mean, *are you* the man? *Am I* the woman, or have we switched, because that's what it feels like.

JONATHAN: No, I think we're just a man and a woman having a conversation.

MARGARET: Yes, but why? Why are we having this conversation, why are we having *any* conversation? Why aren't we tearing each other's clothes off and wearing out my queensized mattress?

(Suddenly there is a loud pounding at the door, followed by grunting.)

MARGARET: What the hell is that?

(Jonathan goes to the door and looks out the peephole.)

MARGARET: Who is it?

JONATHAN: Thank God.

(He opens the door. Lester, a large, drooling man, enters. He carries various

bags of food with him — Chinese take-out, burgers, pizza, etc. Behind him he drags an even larger cooler.)

JONATHAN: Margaret, this is Lester. *(To Lester.)* You know, you could order out after getting here. Some of those places deliver. I was getting desperate.

(Lester grunts in response and makes a grab at Margaret's breasts. Jonathan beats him back.)

JONATHAN: No, no! I haven't told her yet.

MARGARET: *(Covering her chest.)* Told me what?

(Lester moves towards Margaret again. Jonathan pushes him down on to the sofa, reaches into one of the food bags, grabs a burger, unwraps it and puts it into Lester's still-groping hands. Now that Lester is occupied, Jonathan resumes his conversation with Margaret.)

JONATHAN: Um . . . I was getting around to tell you this — there's never really a good time, is there?

MARGARET: You're gay, this is your jealous lover, and going out with me was your attempt at —

(Jonathan gives a nervous laugh.)

JONATHAN: If only things were that simple.

MARGARET: You're bi, going straight?

JONATHAN: No. *(Pause.)*

MARGARET: Well?

JONATHAN: I was born separated from my libido.

MARGARET: What?

JONATHAN: When I was born — at first they thought that Lester and I were twins, fraternal twins. They thought that Lester was retarded, since he only grunted and drooled, even though he seemed to be able to hear and see everything. Then they noticed that I never really took pleasure in eating, while Lester seemed to take nothing *but* pleasure in eating.

MARGARET: Is that why you only ate a salad tonight?

JONATHAN: Exactly. I still get hungry — my body needs food, of course. My stomach rumbles when I'm running low. But in terms of a real desire, a need to taste and savor . . . *(He shrugs.)*

(Lester crumples up his burger wrapper and throws it over his shoulder. Finished, he gets up and starts moving toward Margaret again. Jonathan pushes him back down.)

JONATHAN: Not yet! *(Jonathan reaches into the cooler, pulls out a couple of filled donuts — chocolate covered and cream-filled, powdered and jelly-filled, whatever, the messier the better — and hands them to Lester, who immedi-*

ately begins eating. To Margaret.) Anyway, they discovered through vigilant observation that Lester was my . . . pleasure principle.

MARGARET: *(Faintly.)* Pleasure principle?

JONATHAN: You know — Freud called it the Id. That part of us which derives pleasure from the earthy things, like food and sex.

MARGARET: You waited four dates to tell me about this?

JONATHAN: Well, I thought I could ease into it, once I could tell whether or not you really liked me. And then . . . we both liked Galway Kinnell's poetry and salsa music and . . . and we just connected on so many things . . . I was having such a great time . . . enjoying your company so much, that I was scared to tell you. *(Pause.)* You do like me don't you?

MARGARET: *(Reluctant.)* Yeah.

(Jonathan sits down on the sofa.)

JONATHAN: So . . . now we can start. *(He pats the space next to him.)*

MARGARET: Start?

JONATHAN: Yes. Now that Lester is here, we can start having sex.

MARGARET: Uh, I don't—

JONATHAN: *(Explanatory.)* He's my libido, and now that he's here, we can have sex.

MARGARET: I'm not sure that I —

JONATHAN: I thought you said you liked me —

MARGARET: I do, but —

JONATHAN: I like you too.

(Jonathan stands up and gently kisses Margaret. She responds. Still kissing, Jonathan steers her on to the sofa next to him. Jonathan and Margaret continue making out, Margaret with her eyes closed. Lester watches for a moment, then drops his donut, comes over to them and starts groping Margaret, who doesn't notice — she thinks that it's Jonathan groping her. Lester brings his face closer to them and begins to unbutton Margaret's shirt. Margaret realizes that there are now three hands on her and opens her eyes. Lester lets forth a large belch. Margaret shoves them both away and jumps up from the sofa.)

MARGARET: What the fuck!

JONATHAN: What, did I do something —

(Lester follows Margaret off the sofa and continues to grope her.)

MARGARET: Get him off of me!

JONATHAN: *(Picking up a dropped donut.)* Lester! *(Lester turns to look at Jonathan. Jonathan shoves the donut into his mouth. Thus distracted, Lester temporarily loses interest in Margaret and resumes his seat on the couch, lost in the donut and its scrumptious filling.)*

MARGARET: What was *he* doing?

JONATHAN: Undressing you — I assume you like to have your clothes off during sex.

MARGARET: Why was *he* undressing me?

JONATHAN: Because he's my libido.

MARGARET: Oh my God, you mean that I'm expected to have sex with . . . *that*?

JONATHAN: Well, you're having sex with me, via Lester.

MARGARET: Because he's your libido.

JONATHAN: *(Brightly.)* Right! I knew you'd get it.

(Pause, while Margaret takes in Lester.)

MARGARET: I can't do this.

JONATHAN: If it's hard for you to see that both of us are really me, and that you're actually having sex with just one person, maybe it would help if you thought of this as a threesome. Have you ever fantasized about —

MARGARET: This is *no one's* fantasy!

JONATHAN: But —

MARGARET: I think you had better go.

(Jonathan stands up.)

JONATHAN: You know, I thought you were different, that you were an understanding soul. But now I see that you're just like all the other anti-P.U. women I've been out with.

MARGARET: Anti — P.U.?

JONATHAN: Yes, you're prejudiced against the Psychologically Uncohesive. As a minority group, we try to make strides —

MARGARET: *(Horrified.)* There's more than one of you?

JONATHAN: Yes.

MARGARET: *(To herself.)* Like dating isn't hard enough!

JONATHAN: We're becoming a movement that —

MARGARET: Look — can't you just date a woman with your . . . affliction?

JONATHAN: *(Glumly.)* I can't. P.U. is like color-blindness and hemophilia — women can carry the gene, but only men can have the condition.

MARGARET: Oh. *(Margaret looks at Lester — still occupied with his donut — and gives a shudder of revulsion. Jonathan sees this.)*

JONATHAN: *(Quietly.)* You find me repulsive, don't you?

MARGARET: No, I don't find *you* —

JONATHAN: I just saw the way you looked at Lester. He's a part of me, Margaret. If you find *him* so disgusting, then you find me disgusting too. He can't help the way he looks or acts! He didn't ask to be born all Id, did he?

I'm sorry that you can't find me 100 percent attractive, but we all have parts of us that are less attractive than others. *(Jonathan picks up his coat and puts it back on, with dignity.)* I'm sorry that you can't accept me as I am.

MARGARET: Look, I just . . .

JONATHAN: Come on, Lester.

(Lester looks up from eating. Jonathan nods towards the door. Lester attempts to collect everything but ends up dropping a couple of things, he goes back to grab them.)

JONATHAN: Leave it!

(Lester tries once again to touch Margaret, who jumps back. Jonathan grabs Lester by the collar and tugs him to the door.)

JONATHAN: Goodnight Margaret.

(They exit. Jonathan closes the door. Margaret collapses on the sofa. She notices a large bag of fries has been left on the coffee table. She picks it up, and cautiously takes a bite of the fry. She likes it, grabs a handful and shoves it in her mouth, ravenous. Blackout.)

END OF PLAY

The Right to Remain

MELANIE MARNICH

The Right to Remain premiered at the Mixed Blood Theatre Company, Minneapolis, MN.

CHARACTERS
    AMY, late 30s.
    PETER, late 30s.
    JOSH, midteens.

SETTING
    Their kitchen.

TIME
    The present.

PRODUCTION NOTE
    The Fifth Amendment reads: "Nor shall any person . . . be compelled in
    any criminal case to be a witness against himself." That is, we have the
    right to avoid self-incrimination. That is, we have the right to remain
    silent.

    The Right To Remain was commissioned by Mixed Blood Theatre (Jack
    Reuler, Artistic Director), as one of ten plays for its Bill of (W)Rights
    project, a project designed to explore the state of the Constitution's Bill
    of Rights at the beginning of 2004.

THE RIGHT TO REMAIN

Amy and Josh in the kitchen. Amy is putting dinner on the table. Josh clicks away on a computer in the corner. He never looks away from the screen. Not when he speaks, not when he's spoken to, not until later.

AMY: *(As she puts dinner on the table.)* You OK?

JOSH: Yeah.

AMY: You sure?

JOSH: Yeah.

AMY: You're sure you're sure?

JOSH: Yeah.

AMY: Good.
    (Beat.)

JOSH: What's for dinner?

AMY: Chicken.
    (Josh just grunts.)

AMY: With rice.
    (Just a grunt.)

AMY: And asparagus.

JOSH: Folic acid. Cool. *(Beat.)* Mom?

AMY: Hm?

JOSH: *You* OK?

AMY: Yeah.

JOSH: Cool.
    (Peter enters, just as he ends a call on his cell phone.)

PETER: *(On phone.)* No. No. No. No. No. No. No. OK. Bye. *(He snaps his phone shut.)* I hate my job.

AMY: You have to go back in?

PETER: It can wait till morning.

AMY: That's news.
    (He puts the cell phone on the table and kisses Amy nicely, admiringly, a little flirtatiously.)

PETER: Look at you.

AMY: What?

PETER: You're kind of dressed . . . up.

AMY: A little.

PETER: You look really . . . hot.

AMY: Stop.

PETER: You do.

JOSH: I am in the room.

PETER: Then maybe you should leave.

JOSH: Mom?

AMY: Stay.

PETER: What's the occasion?

AMY: Nothing.

PETER: Not me being home before midnight?

AMY: I had a meeting.

PETER: With who?

AMY: Some guy I might be working with.

PETER: Do I know him?

AMY: Doubt it.

PETER: Should I be jealous?

(*Josh snorts but never looks at Peter.*)

PETER: Shut up. Your mom's gorgeous. And I'm not an idiot.

JOSH: Smell the irony.

PETER: What's that supposed to mean? Huh?

(*Josh shrugs.*)

PETER: Is there any way to slap the teenager out of him?

(*Dinner's on the table. Amy and Peter sit down.*)

PETER: Josh.

(*Josh totally ignores him.*)

PETER: Dinner.

(*Josh ignores him.*)

PETER: Come on.

(*Josh ignores him.*)

PETER: Now.

JOSH: Mom?

AMY: (*To Josh.*) It's OK, hon.

PETER: No, it's not. Get over here. Now.

(*Josh ignores him.*)

PETER: What is it about "now" that you don't understand?

JOSH: Mom?

AMY: I'll warm your food up later.

JOSH: Cool.

PETER: No. Not cool. I mean it.

JOSH: Mom?

AMY: He's working on something.

PETER: Well he can work on it later.

AMY: No he can't.

(Peter's starting to sense that something's up. A weird connection between Amy and Josh that doesn't include him.)

ANY: *(Starting to eat.)* How was your day?

PETER: *(Trying to switch gears.)* Uh, fine. *(Peter starts eating.)*

AMY: Good.

PETER: Busy. Crazy.

AMY: You like that, though. Salt, please.

(He passes it.)

PETER: Yeah. I guess.

AMY: That big account?

PETER: Yeah.

AMY: Who'd've thought snowmobiles could suck up so much time.

PETER: Hey, it's Minnesota. *(To Josh.)* You've got five seconds.

JOSH: Mom?

AMY: *(Sharply, to Peter.)* Leave him alone.

(Now Peter knows something's up. Amy's too benign. Josh is too focused on the computer. It's a tense, bizarre, forced normalcy. A strange current in the room. He tries to feel his way around it.)

PETER: You?

AMY: What?

PETER: Your day. How was it. Including the part about that guy that I don't like the sound of.

(Josh snorts.)

PETER: Do you know how bad I wanna hit him right now?

AMY: My day was fine, thanks.

PETER: You had a huge deadline or something, right?

AMY: Missed it. Does this have too much salt?

PETER: What do you mean you missed it? *(As a command.)* Josh.

(Josh ignores him.)

AMY: I mean five o'clock came and went and I turned in jack shit.

PETER: You never miss a deadline. And you never swear.

AMY: There's a first time for everything. Go fuck a duck.

PETER: Amy?!

AMY: *(Looking directly at him.)* Peter?

(She looks at him until he squirms. For an instant, he's a bunny in the head-lights. Then she looks back at her food.)

PETER: *(Trying to catch his breath after that weird moment.)* So you, like, completely missed it?

AMY: *(Eating.)* Mm.

PETER: Well, that can't be good.

AMY: Pretty bad, actually. The asparagus is limp. Think I'd get it right by now.

PETER: Like "bad" as in "you might get fired" bad?

(No answer. Josh is focused on the computer. Amy's focused on her dinner. The atmosphere is just too weird for Peter.)

PETER: *(Snapping.)* Get off that stupid computer before I throw it out the window. I hate that thing. It's sucking the testosterone out of you. Turn it off. Eat. Then we'll go play football or something.

JOSH: We don't own a football.

AMY: *(Focused on her food.)* Are you online?

JOSH: *(Focused on the computer.)* I can be. Want me to?

AMY: Go ahead.

JOSH: 'Kay.

PETER: You two are starting to freak me out. *(To Josh.)* Come. Here.

AMY: Stay there.

PETER: Come here.

AMY: Stay.

PETER: Come.

AMY: Stay.

PETER: Come.

(Nothing. Josh keeps typing like nothing's happening. Amy keeps eating. Nothing, except for Peter's confusion.)

AMY: Did you remember bread?

PETER: What?

AMY: Bread. I asked you to pick some up.

PETER: I — No. I forgot. I'm sorry. I was really distracted this morning when you asked. I'm sorry.

AMY: I asked yesterday.

(That throws Peter for a loop.)

JOSH: Mom?

AMY: Hm?

JOSH: I'm online.

PETER: Get off.

AMY: Stay on.

PETER: Off!

AMY: On.

PETER: *(Finally losing it.)* Off! You — *(To Amy, who's about to say something.)* stop. And you — *(To Josh.)* get over here.

(They don't react. They don't even blink. It's like they didn't hear him. Whatever the game is, it's becoming clear that Amy and Josh hold all the cards.)

PETER: Are you people insane? You're like a couple of zombies! Who are you? Are you on drugs? What planet are you from? What planet am I on? You were normal this morning. Somebody spill their milk. Somebody burp. Somebody talk about their day and look at me while you're doing it.

(Silence.)

PETER: You're giving me the creeps.

(Finally, Amy looks at him point blank.)

AMY: Three.

PETER: What?

AMY: I said "three."

PETER: Three?

AMY: Two.

PETER: Two what?

AMY: Five. Four.

PETER: What?

AMY: Two.

PETER: Your lottery numbers?

AMY: Nine.

PETER: *My* lottery numbers?

AMY: No.

PETER: A secret code I need to get into the tree house? Because *that* I'd believe right about now.

(Amy just looks at him.)

PETER: Are you OK?

AMY: They're hers, right?

PETER: Whose what?

AMY: The numbers in her phone number.

PETER: The numbers in whose phone number?

AMY: Three-two-five, four-two-nine- What comes after nine? What's the last number of her number?

PETER: Amy —

AMY: Couldn't you come up with a better excuse than "snowmobiles"?

PETER: You mean, my *job?*

AMY: Snowmobile photo shoot, snowmobile trade show, snowmobile convention . . .

PETER: This isn't even worth talking about. It's stupid. It's just . . . *wrong.* Five minutes ago I was jealous of some guy you dressed up for.

AMY: My lawyer.

PETER: What? *(Beat.)* You're crazy.

JOSH: You're busted, dad.

PETER: *(To Josh.)* Shut up. *(To Amy.)* You . . . are . . . so . . . wrong.

AMY: Really?

PETER: You think just because I'm working all the time?

AMY: No. Because you *say* you're working all the time.

PETER: You know I am. I call you from the office. You call me there.

AMY: Cell phones changed the rules. Accessibility doesn't preclude guilt. As a matter of fact, it's the perfect cover.

PETER: What?

AMY: I got that from the lawyer. Pretty good, isn't it?

JOSH: *(Still not looking away from the computer.)* Tell me the last number, dad. Of her phone number.

PETER: There *isn't* one.

JOSH: Yeah there is. And I already know it. Because I called the phone company and got your cell phone records. But I want you to say it. Say it and I'll stop. Two? Seven? Five? One? Nine?

PETER: *(To Amy.)* God, what kind of bullshit is this?

JOSH: If you don't say it, I'll type it in. It'll tell me her name and address. Then I can run a search on her. Credit. Credit cards. Parking tickets. Like that. I can find out where she went to high school. Which means, like, we find out how young she is. If you say the last number, I'll stop. If you admit it. I'll turn off the computer and eat my vegetables at the table next to you. But if you don't, I'll put in the number. I'll find out where you took her for dinner. I can find out days and times. I can find what you bought her. I can find where you stayed. Where you fucked her. How much you paid for the room. Come on. What's the number? Just the last one. Then we can stop. If you admit it.

(Nothing.)

PETER: Why is he . . . ?

AMY: The thing is, I had no idea. He's the one who figured it out. Not me. Not even close. I believed every late night. Every Saturday afternoon. I was thinking "Sure. Why not? Snowmobiles." Because I love you in that really really stupid way. He's pretty smart, though, isn't he? For the son of a stupid mother. Three? Eight? Six?

PETER: Don't do this.

AMY: What's she like?

PETER: There is no —

(To Josh.) Go to your room.

JOSH: Mom?

AMY: Stay.

JOSH: 'Kay.

PETER: God.

(Silence. He doesn't have an ally in the room.)

PETER: It's not.

AMY: It's not what I think it is?

PETER: No. It's not.

AMY: You have no idea what I think.

PETER: *(Holding out his cell phone.)* Here. I'll stand right here while you —

AMY: Don't embarrass yourself.

PETER: No. It's not.

AMY: Don't embarrass yourself.

PETER: Go ahead. Call.

AMY: Don't insult me.

(Beat.)

JOSH: I'm gonna do it now, dad. Unless you say it. *(Josh finally turns to face Peter, dead on. He waits. Nothing.)*

JOSH: What is it about "now" that you don't understand?

PETER: *(Snapping.)* Don't throw my words back in my face! Don't think you're so smart! Don't think for a minute — *(He realizes he's facing his own firing squad.)* Don't.

JOSH: Say "when" Mom.

PETER: Not now. Not in front of him. Not like this.

(No one moves.)

JOSH: Mom?

(Beat.)

PETER: *(Barely.)* Seven.

(Josh gets up from the computer, sits at the dinner table and eats.)

END OF PLAY

Triangle

JANE MARTIN

TRIANGLE

A campus apartment. A young man and young woman sit with their hands in their laps on the sofa.

JOYCE: All right, it's 8:15, she should be here any minute.

ART: I really . . .

JOYCE: Don't even start.

ART: I would never have . . .

JOYCE: But you did.

ART: Joyce.

JOYCE: Shhh.

> *(They sit in silence for a moment.)*

JOYCE: I knew this was coming.

ART: But . . .

JOYCE: *(A warning.)* Arthur.

> *(They wait.)*

JOYCE: This is a classical case. I knew we would have to go through it and I prepared for it. Every relationship faces this . . . or rather, the problem arises when it isn't faced, when it is in fact avoided. We, you and I, are not avoiding it. Are we?

ART: No.

JOYCE: Not all women see this coming but I'm a literature major. It's as old as the written word, it's all over Greek drama.

ART: I only . . .

JOYCE: That's what the male always says, "I only . . ." and then this "only" destroys what was ordained, what was meant to be and the world is the worse for it. Do you know what Homer said about it? He said, "It was always thus."

ART: Homer?

JOYCE: See how lucky you are we hooked up? I know who Homer is, I know who Aeschylus is, I know who they all are. All the way down the line.

ART: It wasn't . . .

JOYCE: It was. It is. This is a "Love Triangle," honey, which is the bed of hot coals over which, barefoot, every committed relationship must walk. We are going to confront this, Arthur, in a way that demonstrates our civility, our resilience, our tensile strength and then we are going on together with our lives. This isn't going to be a bit like Madame Bovary.

(A knock at the door.)

JOYCE: I want you to answer it, Artie. We have the jalapeño cheese plate, the oatmeal cookies and you can offer her wine. All done graciously. We are not going to look back on this with regret.

(He rises and goes to the door where he pauses.)

JOYCE: Go ahead, open it.

(He does. Joyce calls.)

JOYCE: Please come in!

(It is the goddess Aphrodite.)

JOYCE: Well hi, I'm Joyce Renfield Capodice, and of course you're acquainted with Arthur. Not the nicest weather out. I hope you didn't have any trouble finding us?

APHRODITE: None at all.

JOYCE: I'm sorry, I didn't catch your name?

APHRODITE: I am Aphrodite.

JOYCE: Really? That is so pretty. Did you realize you were named after a goddess? Not everyone would know, but I'm a literature major.

APHRODITE: Capodice? Are you Italian?

JOYCE: Why yes, I am.

APHRODITE: Then you should call me Venus. Excuse me for asking, but are you two in love?

ART: Well . . .

JOYCE: Yes, we are . . . deeply.

APHRODITE: That is so delicious. Are you in distress? I'm really drawn to lovers in distress.

JOYCE: Oh, I wouldn't go that far. There is a teeny, tiny confusion that needs clearing up.

APHRODITE: Love's confusion is ambrosial.

JOYCE: Sometimes.

APHRODITE: Or, it isn't love.

JOYCE: Uh-huh. *(Indicated the center of the three-seat sofa.)* Why don't you sit here, Aphrodite, so you'll have access to the cheese tray, Arthur?

ART: Would you like . . .

APHRODITE: I have no digestive tract.

JOYCE: Really? Come and sit, Arthur.

(They sit on either side of Aphrodite.)

JOYCE: Well, here we are.

APHRODITE: We are.

JOYCE: I was telling Art this was a classic lovers triangle. Have you been in a love triangle before?

APHRODITE: Well, there was Zeus and Vulcan.

JOYCE: *(To Art.)* See honey, everybody's gone through it.

APHRODITE: Zeus was also my father.

JOYCE: Well, that's a little more unusual.

APHRODITE: Then I left Vulcan for Mars.

JOYCE: So you know exactly what I'm talking about.

APHRODITE: I do.

JOYCE: All right then, I'm just going to take the bull by the horns here. *(To Arthur who is working on the cheese.)* Honey, don't eat compulsively. Now you met Arthur at the beach?
(Aphrodite smiles.)

JOYCE: Aphrodite, I'm not a jealous person. I don't mind that the two of you talked or that Art spoke of, well, kind of a connection. Oh, I feel we should always be open to connection outside our primary connection. Art and I have a primary connection. We're going to spend our lives together. We are the center, the nexus or as it were, the family. You really ought to try the jalapeño cheese bits. We're shopping for a wedding dress, aren't we, Art?

ART: Well . . .

JOYCE: Together. Maybe something like what you're wearing, only more of it. However, these extra-primary connections need to be stopped short of the "classical triangle" for obvious reasons, don't you agree?
(Aphrodite smiles pleasantly but makes no other sign.)

JOYCE: Now, ummmm . . . what went code red for me was that Arthur mentioned something about a kiss. Aphrodite? Was that a sort of ta-ta-I'll-be seeing-you-kind-of-air-kiss or a . . . well . . . a kiss kiss?

APHRODITE: The horizon line and the water met in a single iridescent blue and when our eyes met, the world exploded in colors you could feel, the very tides ran backward and the zephyred air, warming to our glance, lifted us above the terrestrial sands, ourselves and that which was not ourselves running together until there was no edge, no mortal demarcation and we existed only inside each other, limitless, indistinguishable, screaming with joy.

JOYCE: Uh-huh. But did you kiss.
(Aphrodite shakes her head "no.")

JOYCE: Artie, you scamp! Well for goodness sake he was just trying to make me jealous.

APHRODITE: But his lips enveloped me, and I, as wine for Bacchus, was drawn drunken inside his being, all flow and motion, all ecstasy and forgetting.

JOYCE: Oh, is that so, mister? Well, kiss or no kiss, I'd say that makes this a classical triangle. Darn it to heck!

ART: It was like . . .

JOYCE: I don't care what it was like, Arthur. Dagnab it. Now as a Literature major I can handle this. This absolutely is not out of my league. Every central relationship faces Fol-do-rol like this sooner or later, and sooner is better because there are no little ones involved. Traditionally, whether it's *Anna Karenina* or *Far From the Madding Crowd*, decisions have to be made, choices confronted, and I, Aphrodite, Arthur, choose to be decisive. No triangle in world literature is ever sustained. Arthur, you must choose between us.

ART: Well . . .

JOYCE: Not yet. As in Bernard Shaw's *Candida*, Aphrodite and I will in a civil way, with no more talk of fluids, present from each of our perspectives the case, remembering always that this is a deeply human predicament.

APHRODITE: *(Smiling.)* I'm not human.

JOYCE: Whatever.

APHRODITE: I am a goddess.

JOYCE: I think the applicable term would be home wrecker.

APHRODITE: Lovely mortal, there can be no competition for I wear a magic girdle which renders me irresistible.

JOYCE: Well, you need a girdle, missy. With me what you see is what you get, and what you get with me is hotter than an outdoor grill on the 4th of July. *(To Art.)* Right, baby?

ART: Well . . .

JOYCE: When Artie and I make love, he screams like a parrot, so don't talk to me about liquids. If you ask me, you could use some because, excuse me, I see a lot of cellulite.

(Aphrodite smiles.)

JOYCE: Now that's enough small talk. I'm going first. Arthur, your life, as we both know, cries out for guidance, discipline and security that you are aware I give unselfishly. You need boundaries, Arthur, to flourish. You need to be mastered and I am prepared to make the sacrifices that mastery entails and without that you are, just as miss so-called goddess mentions, nothing but flow, or as I might call it, leakage. I promise you the tough love and criticism and even spanking that will allow you to succeed in Electrical Engineering. I'm in for the long monogamous haul although, as

I have many times said, I prefer to adopt. I will not deviate or waffle or fal-
ter, I will be the gleaming frame that allows your watercolor to exhibit.
This, Arthur, is both who I am and what you, my sweetie, desire. Choose.

ART: Well . . .

JOYCE: Aphrodite?

APHRODITE: Ah. *(Turns to Art.)* What may I offer you, mortal? I am the river
not the bank. I sprang, full-grown, from the foam of the sea near the isle
of Cytherea. I can give only longing, pleasure and the opportunity to become a God, if that's of any interest?

ART: Well gee, I . . .

APHRODITE: We will be met, Arthur, by the Hours, clothed and presented to
the Gods on Mount Olympus where my daughter, the incomparable
Eros, will dance to delight you, and Zephyrus, The West Wind, will cool
your brow as we dine only on Ambrosia and at last, when Phaeton has
driven the chariot of the sun into the deep shadows of evening, I will
bring you the nectar of immortality in a silver chalice and, lying among
the gently enfolding clouds, I will eternally fuck your brains out.

ART: Gee, I think I gotta pick her.

JOYCE: Really? Well frankly, Arthur, I don't care what you do but for God's
sake don't make a speech about it!

ART: OK.

JOYCE: *(Rising.)* Fine. I should have known it. The triangle is always, always a
choice between form and feeling. Feeling doesn't last, Arthur. I don't care
what she says. Licentiousness and nausea are two words for one horrible
reality. I should have never involved myself with you, Artie. I should have
recognized you are inchoate. Good-bye, Aphrodite. Thank you so much
for dropping by. I hope, Arthur, you will have your T-shirts and Benedril
out by the end of the week. I certainly don't mean to rush you both but I
have a test on the love poets of the Victorian era.

APHRODITE: *(Shaking hands.)* Good evening, moral maiden.

ART: *(Shaking hands.)* Bye Joyce.

APHRODITE: Come, my God. *(Puts out her hand. He takes it.)*

ART: OK

*(They exit. Joyce looks after them. She picks up the text she needs to study. A
moment.)*

JOYCE: *(A furious roar.)* Bitch!!!
(Blackout.)

END OF PLAY

178 Head

C. DENBY SWANSON

CHARACTERS
DAG, a farmer.
BEA, his wife.
HARRY, a visitor.

SETTING
A family farm.

178 HEAD

A field.

DAG: 178 head.
> *(A living room: Bea ushers Harry in. She invites him to sit. He smiles. She also sits.)*

BEA: He's out.

HARRY: In the fields?

BEA: Yes.

HARRY: Oh.

BEA: My husband is a farmer, Harry.

HARRY: I know, Bea. So am I, usually.

BEA: I mean, I don't know where else he'd be. In his blood. He can't leave this place. He couldn't leave this place, even if — Even if.

HARRY: If he left the property, there'd have to be a quarantine. It's policy.

BEA: It's almost like the first days of being married, close, so close. Can't leave each other's side. Different reasons, of course.

HARRY: Of course.
> *(Bea casts about for something to do. She exits and returns with two mugs.)*

BEA: Coffee.

HARRY: Thanks.

BEA: It's stale.

HARRY: That's OK.

BEA: No visitors. No vehicles.

HARRY: More good policy.

BEA: So, unless this things travels across phone lines —

HARRY: It got the Wagners' place. Did you hear?

BEA: Yes.

HARRY: Can't be too careful.

BEA: We're fine.

HARRY: Of course.

BEA: We'd call you if we weren't fine. You know we'd make that call.

HARRY: I have a different perspective, Bea. Maybe I could see something that you miss. I just have to look. It's routine.

BEA: Dag will be right in. I'm sure he saw your car.

(A field.)

DAG: 177. My mother lost her words. After supper, she took her plate in. She took my plate, too. 176. She got up and we stayed sitting, our legs stretched out, like hounds, our tough hides splayed open and revealing the thin and tender inner part of the haunch. She walked toward the kitchen. 175. Her legs shook. She stopped. She looked down at herself, surprised at the indignity in these calves now bunched up and bowed in like bolts of fabric, like clumps of embroidery, like the needles themselves. They had walked behind oxen, stalked rabbits, and were now trembling like new grass. They pulled her down into the wood floor that Papa had laid. 174. She turned back to us. She wanted to say something. She opened her mouth and everything peeled off into our hands. Gums. Tongue. Her eyes lolled. The plates crashed. 173. And then it leapt across the room to Uncle Bo, it survived six days in a speck of food on an ocean voyage to the new world, that was the connection and we couldn't even see it, it was invisible and whispery until he got it and it spoke through his mouth, loud, crashing sounds like waves. He drooled until they shot him, and burned him, and then Octavia, who was a sheep, not a mere person, she was the queen of sheep, her loss made my mother sob, made my mother miss her own mother, 172, gaping, 171, everybody sloughing off skin like sheets of paper, 170, and it floated there in the breeze through the kitchen door and out into the garden. All in an afternoon after supper after my mother counted heads and we all came circling in to the clanging of the bell. 169. 168. 167. 166.

(A living room. They sit.)

BEA: The Wagners.

HARRY: Yes.

BEA: Just comes on the air, doesn't it. There's no other explanation.

HARRY: There's a radius around the center of infection. You're in it.

BEA: So are you, now, aren't you?

HARRY: Technically.

BEA: We've been very careful.

HARRY: Everyone has. *(Pause.)* We had to shoot the Wagners' whole herd.

BEA: Everybody?

HARRY: That's the way it works.

BEA: Everybody.

HARRY: Well, it's not like it was the Wagners themselves.

BEA: I think, Harry, I could walk through the pens blindfolded and know each one of my animals by the feel of its hide.

HARRY: You're soft-hearted. Bea.

BEA: That's what Dag says.

HARRY: In a normal year, we'd go to slaughter next week.

BEA: Harry!

HARRY: Not out in the middle of the field where they stand, but orderly, systematic.

BEA: I don't know how you can even talk about that now.

HARRY: That's the way it's supposed to be. Not this —

(Dag enters. He and Harry shake hands.)

DAG: Harry.

HARRY: Dag.

DAG: Saw you drive up.

HARRY: I'm careful with the car. We're trained.

BEA: Next time, Harry, you should call.

HARRY: Call?

DAG: Bea —

BEA: So that I can make fresh coffee.

HARRY: I'm not allowed to warn folks —

BEA: It's just good neighbors, that's all. Can't we be good neighbors anymore?

HARRY: Ask the Wagners.

DAG: I heard it was fast.

HARRY: One minute there was just one and then you turned around and it was suddenly half a dozen, and it was all over you, skin and milk and then the guns, we were out there with them where they stood, white suits, I had to press the gun up against foreheads, more foreheads, another one white, another one white, another one white. They told me they could hear the shots from the house. Three human generations' worth. We burned them and the family came out to say good-bye. They stayed until it was just sparks. Nobody had showed up for Grandmaw's funeral last spring, I guess there had been some sort of falling out.

DAG: I heard.

HARRY: About Grandmaw?

DAG: No. I heard the shots.

HARRY: It's routine. I'll be quick. I was telling Bea.

BEA: He was telling me that I'm soft-hearted.

DAG: Soft heart, thick skin.

BEA: If there was something wrong, we'd call you. We swear.

HARRY: I need to take a look around, Dag.

BEA: We've been very careful. I've scrubbed everything. Haven't I, Dag? I stayed in when they shot those animals, I stayed in and scrubbed everything down.

HARRY: You understand.

DAG: Sure, Harry. I understand.

BEA: Tell me, Harry, who visits your farm?

DAG: Bea. The man's here to take a look at the animals.

HARRY: Aw, Dag. I'm just Harry, like I always am.

BEA: I could hear the shots, too, but I didn't flinch. Not once. If that's not hard-hearted I don't know what is.

DAG: Let him by. *(Dag and Bea stand watching each other.)*

END OF PLAY

Bake Off

S HERI W ILNER

Bake Off premiered at Actors Theatre of Louisville,
Humana Festival of New American Plays, 2002.

CHARACTERS

RITA, age 38–48.

PAUL, age 33–40.

THE PILLSBURY DOUGHBOY, if not available, an actor in costume will do.

SETTING

The "cooking floor" of the Pillsbury Bake-Off.

TIME

1997; one year after the first man won the Grand Prize of the Pillsbury Bake-Off.

BAKE OFF

"Men are making their mark at the Bake-Off Contest. The greatest number of men — fourteen — competed in the 38th contest. *Perhaps, even more significantly, the first Bake-Off finalist to win the $1 million Grand Prize was a man.*"

from Pillsbury Bake-Off website, www.bakeoff.com

Paul is at his portion of the kitchen area unpacking ingredients and supplies from two white boxes. The boxes are marked with the numbers "15" and "16," but the numbers face the audience and out of Paul's view. Paul is wearing the number "15" on his apron.

Rita, wearing an apron marked "16," approaches the kitchen area. She sees Paul and is clearly annoyed. She steps into the kitchen area and Paul sees her.

PAUL: Hi there! I'm number Fifteen. You must be . . . number Sixteen.

RITA: How'd you guess? *(She looks at the equipment and supplies.)* Holy cripes, what did you do?!

PAUL: *(Alarmed.)* I don't know. What? What?

RITA: That's my box. Why the hell did you unpack my box?

PAUL: I didn't know.

RITA: What do you mean you didn't know?

PAUL: It was right here.

RITA: You expect me to believe that?

PAUL: I thought they were both mine.

RITA: Both yours? *(She turns the boxes around to show him the large numbers 15 and 16 printed on each.)*

PAUL: Oh God. Oh my God I'm sorry. Ma'am, I am so sorry.

RITA: You read it off my chest OK. How 'bout directing your eyes to flat surfaces from time to time?

PAUL: No, it's not like that. I'm sorry. I'm so nervous. I didn't even think to turn them around. I'm sorry.

RITA: Aw cripes, you mixed everything together. How much time do we have?

PAUL: Two minutes.

(While Rita speaks, she sorts through the items, placing her ingredients in her area, and Paul's ingredients in his. She could do this with her eyes closed.)

RITA: In 1949 Frances Jerzak from Topeka, Kansas almost got disqualified for bringing her own eggs. This . . . machination of yours would get you booted out of here for sure.

PAUL: Wait. Wait, please. There's got to be a more organized way to do this.

RITA: I'm doing it organized. This is organized.

PAUL: How?

RITA: Process of elimination. Whatever's not mine is yours. *(She picks up a bowl.)*

PAUL: Hold on. That's mine too. I need that. I think. I don't know.

RITA: You don't know?

PAUL: Everything's on paper. Just give me a second. Hold on. *(He takes a recipe card out of his pocket and studies it very carefully.)* Yes. Flour. Right here. See?

RITA: You weren't sure you needed *flour*? This is the Pillsbury Bake-Off.

PAUL: I like to check these things.

RITA: *(Snatching the recipe card from his hands.)* Your secretary type this for you?

PAUL: No. I typed it myself.

RITA: *(Reads.)* "Junior Mint Brownies." Gee, I wonder if you'll need those *Junior Mints* over there?

PAUL: *(Grabbing the card back.)* I would greatly appreciate it if you would move all of the supplies back here to the center.

RITA: This is my stuff.

PAUL: I'm sure it is, but I think we should double-check. Just so there are no misunderstandings during the event. Perhaps I could find an official, someone to oversee what we're doing. Mediate, if you will. *(While he looks around the cooking floor for an official, she begrudgingly moves all the equipment back to the center.)* Thank you.

(They begin to separate their ingredients. Paul is very tense and triple checks everything. Rita finishes quickly and spends the rest of the time observing Paul. When she sees that he is unfamiliar with some of the utensils, her mood alternates between amusement and anger. Paul looks into the bowl of Junior Mints, picks one out and places it off to the side. He notices Rita watching him.)

PAUL: *(Indicating the mint.)* A souvenir. For my son.

RITA: There are four eggs here. How many do you need?

PAUL: Two. Wait. *(He checks his list.)* Yes. I need two.

RITA: So do I. No souvenirs left for junior.

PAUL: Are you sure you need two?

(Rita glares at him.)

PAUL: I'm just asking because now's the time, you know? Once this puppy starts, it starts. We can't yell "time out." Or can we? *(Beat)* Maybe we should request another egg. Can we do that? 'Cause who knows, in the heat of the moment you — or I — may grab one too tightly, or drop it — by accident and then, "BLAM" — "All the king's horses and all the king's men . . ."

(A bell is heard over the loud speaker.)

RITA: Too late. This "puppy" is starting.

VOICE OF ANNOUNCER: Ladies may I have your attention please. Ladies, may —. Excuse me. Ladies *and gentlemen* may I have your attention please.

RITA: Aw, cripes.

VOICE OF ANNOUNCER: Welcome to the 48th Annual Pillsbury Bake-Off.

(Loud cheers resound from the bleachers and cooking floor.)

VOICE OF ANNOUNCER: Our finalists are at their ovens, with their fresh Pillsbury ingredients at the ready, about to prepare America's most scrumptious and creative recipes. But before we begin the competition, we would just like to take a moment to acknowledge a very special VIP in attendance. Seated next to Thomas Barnes, the illustrious CEO of Pillsbury Foods, is Mrs. Betty McBride.

(Rita's jaw drops and she scans the audience.)

VOICE OF ANNOUNCER: At a hundred and two years young, the oldest living winner of the Bake-Off, Ms. McBride won in 1949 for her —

(Rita and the announcer speak simultaneously:)

RITA AND ANNOUNCER: Betty's Apple Brown Betty.

VOICE OF ANNOUNCER: Please take a bow, Ms. McBride.

(Loud sounds of applause are heard. Rita cheers.)

PAUL: *(Holding up a bowl.)* Excuse me, is this flour or baking soda?

RITA: Cripes, have some respect. She's a baking legend.

PAUL: Oh. I . . . I didn't know.

RITA: For your information, there was no "Betty" before that Betty.

VOICE OF ANNOUNCER: OK. Ladies. I mean ladies *and gentlemen* are you ready?

RITA: YES!!

VOICE OF ANNOUNCER: Then start your engines. On your marks . . . get set . . . BAKE!!!

(A loud bell sounds: ding-ding-ding-ding. Rita and Paul begin baking. Paul is as systematic and precise as a scientist. He preheats his oven, triple-checking the temperature. He then coats the bottom of a pan with margarine, painstakingly attempting to apply an even coat. Rita is much looser in her technique, using her hands to scoop out ingredients instead of cups and spoons. She works from instinct, which allows her the ability to look away from what she is doing to eye Paul. At the same moment, they both reach for an egg. Paul smiles at Rita who glares back. They resume baking.)

PAUL: Junior Mints are my son's favorite candy. I figured there are worse things that could go into his brownies, right?

RITA: You know, even if your wife is sick or something, there's still no pinch-hitting allowed.

PAUL: Pinch-hitting? . . . Oh, I get it. No, it's not like that. *I* entered. I was selected. Not my wife. We're divorced. I make these for my son on the weekends. When he comes to visit.

(Rita beings mixing her eggs, aggressively.)

PAUL: Hey, you're splattering —.

RITA: DON'T TALK TO ME!! *(She beats the eggs with increasing violence.)* I knew this would happen. I knew it!

PAUL: Knew what would happen?

RITA: I SAID DON'T TALK TO ME!! *(She adds ingredients to the eggs.)* Last year a man takes home a million dollars — the biggest prize in Bake-Off history and now men everywhere suddenly decide they like making cookies.

PAUL: I'm making brownies.

RITA: Yeah, well you know what I'm making?

PAUL: No.

RITA: "Rita's Unbeata . . . ble Applesauce Pecan Crumb Cake." You think you could make this, Mr. Brownie? Mr. Million Dollar Man?

PAUL: I'm not here for the money.

RITA: The Bake-Off's been around for years . . . there's never, *ever* been a prize so big and "miracle of miracles" it's the first year a man wins. What a random chain of events, huh? What an amazing fucking coincidence!

PAUL: That's not why I'm here.

RITA: You're not going to win. You hear me? You are not going to win.

PAUL: Ma'am, please . . . I can't cook and talk.

RITA: Yeah, and how much have you tried, Mr. Suddenly Single?

(An actor enters dressed in a Pillsbury Doughboy costume. He pushes his hands into his stomach and gives the doughboy laugh.)

THE PILLSBURY DOUGHBOY: He-hee. Is everybody making friends?

RITA: This isn't right. He shouldn't be allowed here. I bet this is the only thing he's ever baked.

THE PILLSBURY DOUGHBOY: He-hee. Everyone can bake. Baking is fun.

RITA: Oh yeah, it's a real roll in the hay.

THE PILLSBURY DOUGHBOY: Nothin' says lovin' like somethin' from the oven. He-hee. Happy baking! *(The Pillsbury Doughboy exits.)*

PAUL: Guess that's the final word. You can't go any higher up than him.

RITA: How many dinners for your family have you ever cooked?

PAUL: What does that have to do with this?

RITA: EVERYTHING! It has everything to do with this, Mr. Making-A-List-And-Checking-It-Twice. It must be nice to play in the kitchen only when you want to. Most of us were assigned kitchen duty without having any say in the matter.

PAUL: Look lady, I don't know how else to say this. You're bothering me.

RITA: Oh, you poor man. Is making forty percent more than the women who have the same job as you getting to be too much of a strain?

PAUL: Shit! One-quarter cup butter, not one-third! Don't talk to me anymore. OK? No talking.

RITA: *(With contempt.)* Brownies.

(They return to their preparations. Rita combines another set of ingredients. Paul stirs his melted mints. Having made one error, he is now even more cautious. His anxiety drives Rita crazy, and in their preparations a direct correlation develops between his level of nervousness and her level of violence until he finally explodes:)

PAUL: Please stop it! STOP IT! You're scaring the shit out of me!!

RITA: Hey, if you can't take the heat . . .

PAUL: I can take the heat. It's you I can't take.

RITA: How old's your son?

PAUL: Thirteen. Why?

(Rita looks out into the audience.)

RITA: I want to know where he's sitting.

PAUL: That's none of your business.

RITA: How's he like having his dad in the Pillsbury Bake-Off? You his new hero?

PAUL: I'm trying to be. If you really must know, I am trying to be a hero. His kind of hero.

RITA: His kind of hero? What does what mean?

PAUL: What decade are you living in? This is not 1949. Times have changed. Men cook now. Some of the most famous chefs are men.

RITA: *All* of the most famous chefs are men. Women who cook well get to have Thanksgiving at their house every year. Men who cook well run five-star restaurants and get their pictures pasted on bottles of over-priced sauces.

PAUL: Please, he's watching us. I don't want him to think there's anything wrong with this —

RITA: Yeah, well maybe there is something wrong with this and maybe I want him to know.

PAUL: Ma'am, please, I'm appealing to you as a parent. Do you have children?

RITA: Five.

PAUL: Well mine thinks there's something wrong with him. Mine is losing everything that's special and good about him because he's trying to squeeze through some ridiculous mold that he doesn't fit through. I'm here to show him that I'm proud of who he is. That all I'll ever want from him is that he be true to himself. That he accepts himself. So please, I beg you, let me do that.

RITA: Lucky for you your son didn't need his little ego boost a couple of years ago. Then you would have only won fifty thou.

PAUL: I'll tell you what, if you leave me alone, and I win, you can have the million dollars. That's not why I'm here —

RITA: I don't want your million dollars. I am more capable than you will ever be of winning that million dollars. I have been baking my whole life, not just when my son developed a pre-pubescent crisis.

PAUL: It's more than a pre-pubescent — Why am I arguing with you? I am not the only man in this contest. Why don't you start picking on the other guys and leave me alone?

RITA: There are no other men in this contest.

PAUL: Yes there are. There are five to be exact. *(He points across the cooking floor.)* Look right there, there's one, at Oven fifty-four.

(Rita scans the rows of contestants.)

RITA: Holy shit. You assholes are everywhere!! Hey you! Number fifty-four! Hey fifty-four, I'm talking to you! *(She reaches for an egg and goes to hurl it in the direction of Oven 54.)*

PAUL: That's mine! *(Paul grabs the egg out of her hands.)* What is the matter with you?!

RITA: This is what they give us. *This. (She spreads open her arms to indicate the cooking floor.)* Why do you want it, huh? *(She stands up on the counter.)*

PAUL: Jeez, lady, get down.

RITA: Why do you want this? *(She looks all around the cooking floor.)* This is quite a kingdom, isn't it? This is quite the fucking kingdom. *(Shouting out to Oven 54.)* What's the matter? You tired of running Fortune 500 companies? You tired of sitting in your Congressional seats and ruling countries? Now you'd rather have this? *This?!* Well you can't have it. You hear me? YOU CAN'T HAVE IT! They give this to us and as much as it reeks and stinks to high heaven this is what is ours and you're not going to get your fucking hands on it. *(To Paul.)* Tell that to your son. Wherever the hell he is. *(She scans the audience.)* Where are you Junior? Where are you? Ah, there you are.

PAUL: Stop it!

RITE: This isn't yours. You hear me? Stay away!

PAUL: Please. Stop. He's only thirteen. Please. *(Paul calls out to his son.)* It's OK, Billy. Everything's OK.

RITA: Everything is not OK. Your being here is NOT OK. *(To the child.)* THIS IS NOT OK, BILLY!

(The Pillsbury Doughboy enters, running.)

THE PILLSBURY DOUGHBOY: Is there a problem here?

RITA: Is there a problem here? Yes. There is a big problem here.

THE PILLSBURY DOUGHBOY: He-hee. SECURITY!

RITA: You scared of me, Doughboy? Huh? You scared of me? What kinda boy are you? Show some dough balls, why dontcha? You got dough balls, Doughboy? Where are they? *(She pokes him in the stomach.)*

THE PILLSBURY DOUGHBOY: He hee!

(She pokes him again, lower.)

RITA: Here?

THE PILLSBURY DOUGHBOY: He hee! Help!

RITA: Here? Where are they? What part of this marshmallow body proves that you're a boy? If you got something, show it, Doughboy.

THE PILLSBURY DOUGHBOY: Security!

RITA: Are women supposed to be attracted to you? Are you supposed to be some kind of sex symbol? OK then. *(She grabs the Doughboy's head and begins kissing and fondling him. The Doughboy makes Doughboy-sounding struggling noises and tries to push her away.)* Yum. You taste good, Doughboy. You taste good. Not quite done yet though. Ten more minutes at 350 I think.

(Paul pulls her away.)

PAUL: Leave him alone.

THE PILLSBURY DOUGHBOY: *(Husky, masculine voice.)* Crazy bitch.

RITA: What?

(The Pillsbury Doughboy removes the head of his costume.)

THE PILLSBURY DOUGHBOY: You heard me, keep your paws to yourself you crazy bitch.

PAUL: *(To the Doughboy)* Now wait a minute.

RITA: AGGHHH! *(She throws everything on the counter down onto the floor.)*

THE PILLSBURY DOUGHBOY: Holy shit!

PAUL: Lady — Rita, please. It's OK Billy, just a little accident. Everything's fine.

THE PILLSBURY DOUGHBOY: Hey, we need a cleanup here! Cleanup at 15 and 16.

RITA: Mrs. McBride, where are you? Where are you, Mrs. McBride?

THE PILLSBURY DOUGHBOY: *(While putting his head back on.)* It's gonna be a long fucking day. *(To Paul.)* Thanks for everything, pal. *(The Pillsbury Doughboy shakes Paul's hand. Rita turns around and sees this. The Doughboy speaks, pointedly to Paul, in the Doughboy voice.)* I hope you win. Hee hee! *(The Pillsbury Doughboy fraternally slaps Paul on the back and then exits. Paul looks at Rita.)*

PAUL: I'm sorry. I — *(Beat.)* What a putz, huh?

RITA: This is ours. *(Out to Mrs. McBride.)* Mrs. McBride, tell them this is ours. Mrs. McBride, Betty, tell them this is ours.

END OF PLAY

PLAYS FOR
FOUR ACTORS

The Human Voice

CARLYLE BROWN

The Human Voice was commissioned by
and premiered at the Guthrie Theater,
Joe Dowling, Artistic Director.

CHARACTERS

THE HUMAN VOICE
A MAN
HIS WIFE
AN AUTOMATED TELEPHONE OPERATOR

SETTINGS

Bedroom of the Human Voice.
Garden terrace of a New York apartment.

TIME

Now.

THE HUMAN VOICE

Lights up.

The Human Voice is camped out in her bed. A bed of chaos, filled with lots of fluffy pillows, a carton of cigarettes, an over-filled ashtray, empty food wrappers, Chinese take-out containers, and a stack of popular magazines. An end table near the head of the bed, holds a lamp, a clock, three bottles of champagne (two empty, one full), three or four bottles of pills, and a telephone receiver with the portable handset missing.

The Human Voice lies in her bed inert and waiting.

The telephone rings.

HUMAN VOICE: Finally . . . Where is it? Where is it? Where's the fucking telephone? Oh God, don't let him hang up . . . I'm coming . . . Please, don't hang up . . . I'm coming . . . Please baby, don't hang up. *(Finally she finds the telephone nestled among her pillows. She turns it on.)* Hello . . . Hello . . . Shit! Shit! Shit! Why didn't I leave the phone on the receiver? I'm so fucking stupid. I should have left the phone on the goddamn receiver. *(She turns off the phone and pushes the button on the receiver's answering machine.)*

THE HUMAN VOICE'S VOICE: "I'm sorry, I can't get to the phone right now, but if you will leave a brief message, I'll get back to you as soon as I can."
*(There is a beep and then silence. She turns the phone on again, dials *69, and listens.)*

AUTOMATED OPERATOR: "The number calling cannot be reached at this time. Please hang up now."
(The Human Voice turns off the phone, turns it on again, dials a number and she listens.)

AUTOMATED OPERATOR: "Your call cannot be completed as dialed. Check the number and try again."
(The Human Voice turns off the phone and sits in her bed in a distracted despair. Suddenly the telephone rings. The Human Voice turns on the telephone.)

HUMAN VOICE: Hello? Hello . . . Is it you? I can't hear you . . . I said I can't hear you very well. It's difficult to hear you. You sound so far away . . . Hello . . . Oh, this is awful . . . It sounds as if there're other voices . . . Other voices. . . .What? . . . Yes, try again . . . I said, hang up and try again. I'll be here. Call me right back OK? *(She turns the phone off and puts it in her lap. She watches the phone and she waits. The telephone rings. The Human Voice turns the telephone on.)* Oh, at last it's you. Are you on your cell phone? . . .But it sounds like you're on you're cell phone . . . What? . . . I'm fine. No problems here. And how are you? Are you OK? . . . Are you sure? . . . You didn't call me earlier, did you? . . .There's no need to apologize, I know it's not the usual time, but it's never too late for you to call me . . . I say it's never too late. Any time, day or night, I always long to hear the sound of your voice . . . Yes, your voice . . . What? . . . Please, don't say that. Don't spoil things. How can it be a night like any other night when I'm never going to see you again? . . . No, I just came in . . . only a few minutes ago . . . I went out to dinner . . . Where? I went to La Palma. Where else would I go? You weren't here and I missed you so much. I wanted to be in a place where we had been together . . . Yes, I'm a romantic, but you already know that . . . No, I haven't gotten undressed yet . . . What am I wearing? I'm wearing that white linen dress with the zipper up the back that you like so much, because you say it shows off my hips, and slips off so easy . . . Yes, of course I'm going to take it off, I'm going to bed . . . No, darling, not tonight, please. I just want to talk. To hear the sound of your voice . . . Well all right, if you insist . . . No I want to, really I do. It's so sexy when you talk to me that way. Undressing me with your voice . . . I'm unzipping it now. It's just falling to the floor. Bra, gone, panties, gone, I'm naked, bare, thinking of you, touching myself, getting lost in the sound of your voice . . . Yes, I know this is hard for you too . . . But I do try to be understanding, don't I? . . . Oh no, don't say it . . . You're so sweet. Of course I love you . . . I love you more than you'll ever know . . . I said, more than you'll ever know. *(Crossfade. A garden terrace of a New York apartment. The Man is on a cell phone.)*

MAN: I know. I know you do. And you know I love you too, don't you? . . . Good. Good. I don't know what I'd do if you thought I didn't . . . No, no, I'm all right. I'm fine. Really . . . It's just the same as usual. Working myself to death . . . What? . . . Cell phone? . . . No, I'm not on the cell phone. I'm at the office . . . You can hardly hear me because this phone system is a fucking mess. You can't even get a human voice anymore, just a lot of automated crap. Use a cell phone you get cancer in your ear. It's all fucked up . . . No, I won't work too late. . . .What can I do? I have to work. I'm almost finished just now, getting ready to go . . . go to the house . . .

(Crossfade.)

HUMAN VOICE: Just go ahead and say it. Home. You're going home . . . But it is your home, and I don't like you saying it isn't . . .You're just punishing yourself, and when you get guilty like that you start to lie to me, and you don't tell me the truth . . . No, no, not in that way. . . . I don't mean lying in that way . . . What way? I don't mean in a mean way. You only lie to protect me, to spare my feelings . . . But don't you see, what you say is so important to me now, because all I have left is the sound of your voice. First we don't see each other anymore and then one day you'll hang up the telephone, and I'll be left with nothing but the silence, no voice in my ear to hold me, touch me . . .

(Crossfade.)

MAN: You know, sometimes when you talk like this you make me feel as if I were losing my mind. Like a great silence was growing inside of me. I can't speak, I don't know what to say, my brain is a blank. I feel like I'm going to pass out at any minute . . . No, I'm not blaming you. It's me. My fault. I just don't know how to do this . . . This! I don't know how to do this! . . . I'm sorry. I didn't mean to yell at you . . . No, I'm not angry . . . Really . . . Yes really . . . I promise . . . I swear . . . Please don't cry. Please don't. . . . I can't hear you . . . Calm down . . . Calm down, I'm right here. Can you hear my voice? You can't hear it if you're crying. Aren't there tissues by your bed? . . . Well, take a tissue and wipe your eyes . . . Please, do that for me . . . Good girl . . . All done? . . . Now blow your nose . . . I'm not being condescending. I just want you to stop crying, to stop being sad, to be all right . . .

(Crossfade.)

HUMAN VOICE: I know. I know that's what you want . . . You know me, just be-ing dramatic, morbid . . . I knew exactly what I was doing. I shouldn't feel guilty and you shouldn't take the blame. Our love was up against so many things, and we had to fight against them all the time. But you took care to soothe me and open my eyes. I knew what I was doing, and I don't regret any of it. Not one single minute in all those years. They were priceless. Now, I'm determined to be brave, and I will. I've stopped crying, I hear your voice, and I'm all right. . . .Who's making it up? . . . Who is? . . . Am I making it up? . . . How could I? . . . I haven't got it in me. You know what I'm like. . . . But, you could tell by my voice. It isn't the voice of someone trying to hide something. I didn't think I could be so strong, but I am you know . . . Well, don't admire me too quickly. Maybe I won't be so brave tomorrow when I'll never see you, the way I see you now in my mind, as if I had eyes in the place of ears . . . Yes, I can see you now. You're wearing those smart Italian shoes, a very sporty, loose fitting suit, blue, with the sleeves rolled up, and one of your big, over-sized fluffy shirts, that make you look so sexy, open at the neck, with your tie hanging down untied. You're at your desk with your receiver in your left hand and with your right you're sketching on a legal pad, faces, stars, doodles . . .

MAN: . . . Doodles?

HUMAN VOICE: . . . Am I right?

MAN: . . . Yes, you're exactly right.

HUMAN VOICE: . . . I thought so.

MAN: . . . I'm imagining you too, you know?

HUMAN VOICE: . . . No please, whatever you do, don't imagine me. I don't even look at myself in the mirror anymore. When I do, I find myself looking at just a plain woman, with ordinary hair and sad eyes . . .

MAN: . . . But I love your hair. You've got beautiful eyes, a remarkable face.

HUMAN VOICE: . . . There's nothing remarkable about it. What could be worse? Remarkable faces are for actors. I'd rather hear you say, "My little monkey face. Where is my little monkey face?"

MAN: . . . Don't talk about yourself that way.

HUMAN VOICE: . . . I was just joking . . .

MAN: . . . I don't like it . . .

HUMAN VOICE: . . . A joke.

MAN: . . . I thought you told me you were going to be brave.

HUMAN VOICE: . . . Sometimes baby, you're not very clever, but still you love me. If you were just being clever and didn't love me, this telephone would be like a weapon, beating me with its sound.

(The Wife enters. The man quickly turns off his cell phone and puts it in his pocket.)

HUMAN VOICE: Hello . . .

(The Man and Wife embrace and kiss.)

HUMAN VOICE: Hello . . .

(The Man and Wife stand holding each other.)

HUMAN VOICE: Hello . . .

(Lights out on the garden terrace.)

HUMAN VOICE: Are you there? Can you hear me? *(The Human Voice shuts off the phone, and puts it between her legs in the bed. She watches it, like wait-*

ing for water to boil. She picks it up, turns it on again and dials a number . . . We hear an official ringing.)

AUTOMATED OPERATOR: "You have reached the offices of the Cocteau Corporation. Our office hours are between nine and five, Monday through Friday. If you know the extension of the person you are calling, you may enter it at any time during this message . . ."

(The Human Voice enters an extension number.)

THE MAN'S VOICE: "I'm either on another line, or away from my desk. Leave a message and I'll get back to you as soon as I can."

AUTOMATED OPERATOR: At the sound of the tone, please leave a message, or dial zero for more options . . ."

(The Human Voice shuts off the phone. She dials another number. We hear a hollow ringing.)

AUTOMATED OPERATOR: "The party you are calling has either turned off their cell phone, or is out of reach of the calling area. Please leave a message or try again later . . ."

(There is a beep.)

HUMAN VOICE: We were cut off. What happened? Please, call me back as soon as you can. I'll be waiting. *(She shuts off the phone. Crossfade. Garden terrace. The cell phone beeps.)*

THE WIFE: You have a voice mail. Aren't you going to answer it?

MAN: I don't want to talk to anyone tonight.

THE WIFE: But it might be the babysitter. Answer.

(The Man takes out his cell phone and listens to the voice mail.)

THE WIFE: What is it?

MAN: It's my secretary. I have to talk to this guy about this business deal tonight. Right now in fact. Would you excuse me for a minute?

THE WIFE: No. You said you didn't want to talk to anyone. I only wanted to answer the phone, because I thought it was the babysitter. Talk to whoever it is later. Why don't you talk to me for once.

(Lights up. The Human Voice is on the phone. The cell phone rings. The Wife takes the cell phone from the Man and answers it.)

THE WIFE: Hello . . .

(The Human Voice shuts off her phone . . . Lights out on the Human Voice.)

THE WIFE: That was her, wasn't it? . . . You haven't told her? . . . Why haven't you told her? If you did she doesn't seem to know it . . . I'm fighting for my life here, my home, my family . . . You call her now and you tell her, or don't come home . . . And you be kind to her . . . God knows that could be me.

(The Wife exits. The Man dials his cell phone. The phone rings. Lights up on the Human Voice. Lights out on the Man.)

HUMAN VOICE: Thank God it's you. What happened? We were cut off . . . Yes, I know the telephone system is all fucked up. Listen to me baby; I never told you an untruth have I? . . . Yes, I believe you . . . I do . . . It's that I've been lying to you . . . Me, over the telephone, just now . . . Look, I know there's nothing left to hope for, but lying isn't going to change anything, and besides, I don't like lying to you. I won't, not even for your sake . . . I wasn't telling the truth when I said I went to La Palma. I haven't been anywhere. I'm not wearing a white linen dress. I'm in my underwear just sitting here watching the phone, waiting for it to ring. If you hadn't called me back, I would have died . . . Listen, I know this must be unbearable for you, but I'm suffering here. This fucking telephone is the only connection we have left. Before when we could see each other and we had problems, a look in each other's eyes would change everything. But on the telephone there's no way to know what's the truth . . . Well, supposing you were lying to me now, to make our break-up less painful . . . I'm not saying you are, but if you were lying and I knew it . . . For example, if you weren't at the office, and you told me you were. And maybe you were with her now, and you didn't want to tell me, because you don't want to hurt me. Didn't want me to feel as if I was something you did in between things . . . Because it's hard being the other woman, Thanksgiving, Christmas, all the holidays, Sundays, every day that matters, you're alone. You do it because you have to, but it's not what you really want . . . Don't pity me. Please, for God's sake, don't pity me . . . No . . . No! It would be like losing you over and over again. Nothing but a life of good-byes, why delude myself, it's over . . . Please, don't . . . I want to keep the memories too . . . Don't do this . . . Don't . . . It's always that little boy in you, the one who needs me so much, that charms me and makes me weak. He always comes out just before you hang up the phone. . . . I can tell by your voice . . . I said I could tell by the sound in your voice . . . Listen, you've got to help me here. I can't do this by myself . . . Just listen to me. I want you to do one last thing for me. I want you to do it because you love me . . . I want you to hang up . . . Now . . . Please, be brave for my sake . . . Break off quickly . . . Hang up. Hurry. I love you . . . I love you . . .

(She hears the sound of a dial tone.)

HUMAN VOICE: I love you . . .

(Blackout.)

END OF PLAY

Hurry!

BRIDGET CARPENTER

To Dina

Hurry! was commisioned by and premiered at the Guthrie Theater,
Joe Dowling, Artistic Director.

HURRY!

A young woman sits at a table. The tabletop has a folded card with the letter G on it. She's in the middle of a cell phone call.

WOMAN: Yes I'm here. I *said* I would do it and I'm doing it. Yeah. Right. I'll let you know.

(Woman hangs up. We hear: DING! The Speed Date Leader has rung her bell — the kind on motel desks — and is now waiting expectantly for attention from the group. She speaks into a microphone.)

SPEED DATE LEADER: *(On the mic.)* People, let's focus, we've got a lot of dating to do in the next hour. Welcome to "Make Your Move," Speed Dating for Finicky Urban Professionals. OK. Focus! Here's how it works. Each lady has her own table and a list of her dates. The men *move;* the ladies *stay put.* Ladies, *let the men come to you.* You have *two minutes* per date. Pay attention to the bell. Hurry up and *Make Your Move!*

(Ding! A Guy sits down with the woman.)

WOMAN: Hi.

GUY: Hi.

WOMAN: Have you, . . . done this before?

GUY: Oh yeah. This is my eleventh time.

WOMAN: Eleventh?

GUY: Yeah.

WOMAN: Wow. So — I guess. Wow. Speed dating. It's fun, right?

GUY: *(Pointedly.)* It is when you *play by the rules.*

WOMAN: What, what do you mean.

GUY: That paper they gave you, it has topics for *conversation, questions.*

WOMAN: Oh. *(She glances at the paper.)* You don't want to just talk?

GUY: We *can.* *(Pause.)* The questions are interesting though.

WOMAN: I'll ask a question. How about that. *(She consults the paper. Reads.)* "Have you ever seen a ghost?"

GUY: No.

(Pause.)

WOMAN: "Do you believe in ghosts?"

GUY: No.

(Pause.)

WOMAN: These are kind of stupid questions.

GUY: They're *ice breakers.* They're not designed to be about *intelligence.* Why are you doodling. Are you bored?

WOMAN: No no, um doodling just makes me feel more relaxed, I guess, more comfortable.

GUY: Because I'm making you uncomfortable.

WOMAN: No no not at all. I just doodle. You are making me a little uncomfortable.

GUY: It's because I'm a mathematician. Numbers make people uncomfortable.

WOMAN: I don't think so, I didn't have any idea that you were a —

GUY: *(Interrupting on "idea.")* Let's start over.

WOMAN: Um.

GUY: Let's start over.

WOMAN: OK . . .

GUY: What are your hobbies? Do you have any brothers or sisters? What's your favorite color? Where were you born? What kind of music do you like? If you could be any animal, what would you be? What's your favorite way to spend a Sunday afternoon? When do you get up in the morning? What do you like best, Mexican, Italian, or Chinese? What's in your refrigerator? If you could be anywhere on earth right now, where would you be? *(Ding!)*

SPEED DATE LEADER: *(On the mic.)* Make Your Move! Next! Let's go! Hurry hurry hurry!

GUY: OK, nice to meet you.

(He exits. Dude enters, sits down with Woman.)

DUDE: Hey.

WOMAN: Hi.

DUDE: I get to sit at the G-spot! *(Laughs heartily.)* I FOUND THE G-SPOT! Get it?

WOMAN: Got it.

DUDE: I'm number two, hope that doesn't mean I'm through! *(Laughs heartily.)*

WOMAN: Uh, no.

DUDE: You seem a little shellshocked, sweetheart.

WOMAN: I guess I haven't gotten the hang of this yet.

DUDE: The speed?

WOMAN: Right, the speed.

DUDE: I love it, man. Speed dating. I love the efficiency, I love the adrenaline rush, I love that it's *survival* of the *speediest* — I think it's awesome. Thirty dates in an hour — POW. BOOM.

WOMAN: That's a positive attitude.

SPEED DATE LEADER: *(Coming over to them; off the mic.)* I'm interrupting for *(Checks watch.)* ten seconds. I always like to give a few couples a racy little topic to respond to — just to throw something *wild* into the conversational mix! For instance: "waxing" — discuss!
(She laughs merrily and leaves them.)

WOMAN: *(Laughs halfheartedly.)*

DUDE: Waxing? Like, the hair on my ass? Only if I was *Greek*! *(Laughs heartily.)*
(Pause.)

WOMAN: I'm Greek.
(Pause.)

DUDE: I've been to Greece.

WOMAN: Uh huh.

DUDE: So wow, you don't have a huge hooked *nose* . . .

WOMAN: What?!

DUDE: Yeah I was in Greece. Anyway. You look way, way familiar.

WOMAN: I'm not.

DUDE: I feel like I've seen you before.

WOMAN: You haven't.

DUDE: I feel like I know you.

WOMAN: You don't.

DUDE: You're not my *dental hygenist* are you?? *(Laughs heartily.)*

WOMAN: No.

DUDE: Ha, ha. My Big Fat Greek Dental Hygenist. SEQUEL! Ha. So what do you do?

WOMAN: What do *you* do?

DUDE: I'm an engineer.

WOMAN: Really.

DUDE: I design shit that they use in the space program.

WOMAN: Wow.

DUDE: So I'm one of the few people actually *qualified* to say, "Hey, that isn't rocket science!" *(Laughs heartily.)* Because you know rocket science is *what I do!* So I'd *know* if something wasn't it! Come on tell me what do you do.

WOMAN: *(Reluctant.)* I'm an actress.

DUDE: No shit! I knew it! I knew it! I've seen you in something.

WOMAN: No you haven't.

DUDE: I HAVE. I HAVE. A movie. What movie? What the shit was it? It's on the tip of my tongue! Or, or some TV show . . .

WOMAN: No. Neither. I just do theater.

(Pause.)

DUDE: Really?

WOMAN: Yes.

DUDE: Theater? Like, plays?

WOMAN: Right.

DUDE: Are you in a play here in town?

WOMAN: Yes.

DUDE: Right now? You're in a play right now.

WOMAN: Yes.

DUDE: That is so fucking cool. What's the play? Do you like it?

WOMAN: It's a trifle.

DUDE: What's that mean?

WOMAN: It doesn't mean anything. I mean the play doesn't mean anything.

DUDE: Oh come on. Everything means something.

WOMAN: This doesn't.

(Ding!)

SPEED DATE LEADER: *(In the mic.)* Make Your Move! Next! Hurry hurry hurry!
HURRY!

(Dude exits. No one comes to sit down. The woman makes a cell phone call.)

WOMAN: Are you there? Pick up if you're there. *(Pause.)* OK I just wanted to
call and tell you that I hate you. Thanks for recommending this.

(She hangs up. The Guy from before sits down at the table.)

GUY: Were you bored talking to that guy?

WOMAN: Um . . . didn't we already have a, a date?

GUY: Tonight there are quite a few more women here than men. I didn't want
you to be sitting alone. So I came back.

WOMAN: Won't that, um, mess up things for the other women at other tables?

GUY: I've been here eleven times. I know how to work the system.

WOMAN: Oh.

(Pause.)

GUY: So were you bored with the second guy? Or uncomfortable? I didn't see
you doodling, that's why I ask.

WOMAN: I uh, I don't really want to answer that, I don't think.

GUY: Because you're uncomfortable.

WOMAN: Yeah.

GUY: *Damn!* Dammit, dammit, I always *do* this!

WOMAN: It's not you, it's me.

GUY: Really?

WOMAN: Sure.

GUY: Whew. Great. So what were you guys just talking about?

WOMAN: You know, I'm sorry. I made a mistake. I shouldn't have come here.

GUY: Why?

WOMAN: I don't know. I'm just, very, very uncomfortable.

GUY: But you said that was you.

WOMAN: I'm going to leave.

GUY: Wait for the bell. Please. If you leave right now they'll know I didn't move in the right order.

WOMAN: OK. Fine.

(Pause. They sit. She almost doodles, then stops herself.)

WOMAN: Why have you come here eleven times?

GUY: I work with numbers. I don't have many opportunities to meet people. As a mathematician, I appreciate the odds. Why are you here?

WOMAN: I promised my friend Dina that I'd go.

GUY: Why does she care?

WOMAN: My fiancé died two years ago and I haven't been on a date since then. That's why. *(Little pause.)* I was with someone, and we were in love, and then he died, and boom I was alone. It happened that fast.

(Dude comes over.)

DUDE: Hey guy, you're screwing up the order. Is he bothering you? You're not supposed to be here.

GUY: Why don't you just focus on your own Speed Schedule.

DUDE: Why don't you take your pocket protector and shove it up your —

(Ding!)

SPEED DATE LEADER: *(On the mic.)* Is there a problem over at Table G. *(Speed Date Leader comes over.)* I don't see you two gentlemen *hurrying.* Ladies H through Z are *waiting.* The key word in this organization is SPEED. As in Road Runner. Beep beep! *(Pause.)* Is there a problem?

GUY/DUDE: No.

SPEED DATE LEADER: *(Gesturing.)* Beep beep.

(The men exit.)

SPEED DATE LEADER: Hold tight, dear. Someone'll get to you in a flash.

(Speed Date Leader returns to her bell. Woman sits alone. Her phone rings.)

WOMAN: Hi. I'm still here. I didn't mean to hurt your feelings. Well OK I did but not permanently. This is completely weird and I've only talked to two guys so f —

GUY: Is that Dina?

WOMAN: I'll call you back.

GUY: They took me out of the lineup. I have to start over. I think this person is new, she's not very organized. You didn't leave.

WOMAN: No.

GUY: Did I overhear you say that you were in a play.

WOMAN: I, I really don't want to talk about that.

GUY: How come.

WOMAN: People always think that acting is more interesting than it is.

GUY: *(Resignedly.)* No one ever thinks that about math.

WOMAN: Plus the play, OK I'm not a playwright but I don't think there's very much there.

GUY: How so.

WOMAN: It's just — small. It doesn't feel like it's saying anything.

GUY: What's it about?

WOMAN: It's about a date. That's it.

GUY: That's not so small.

WOMAN: It's about as small as it gets.

GUY: Maybe it's small, but it's precise. I mean a date is basically two variables within a fixed situation, and the variables want to change. Inasmuch as variables "want" anything. Right?

WOMAN: Right . . .

GUY: With math it's funny, you look at numbers for a really long time. You wait. You don't understand the equation, and you just — wait. There's no hurrying understanding. So you keep waiting, numbers in front of you, and then one day — suddenly — you *understand.* The variables have *shifted.* The equation *changes.* More accurately, your *perception* of the equation changes. And it's happened so fast you can't even compute the speed.

WOMAN: You sit and stare at numbers until they change.

GUY: That's right.

WOMAN: How long does it take?

GUY: Depends. I had one theorem, took me three years.

WOMAN: That's a long time.

GUY: Then, boom.

WOMAN: Boom.

(Ding! Woman and Guy stare at one another.)

END OF PLAY

Now We're Really Getting Somewhere

KRISTINA HALVORSON

Now We're Really Getting Somewhere was commissioned by
and premiered at the Guthrie Theater,
Joe Dowling, Artistic Director.

CHARACTERS

JEN, mid 20s. Cynical, unhappy.

BETHANY, mid 20s. Unhappy, trying hard not to be.

ELAINE, late 20s. Jen and Bethany's supervisor, trying hard in general.

JACK, late 20s. Sales guy. Nice enough.

SETTING

At work.

TIME

Today.

NOW WE'RE REALLY
GETTING SOMEWHERE

Lights up on a conference table. Jen is waiting for someone. Bethany walks in and proceeds to pile tons of office crap on the table — files, legal pads, water bottle, Diet Coke, coffee — is she here for a three-day summit? They barely look at each other, having already gone through their morning greetings earlier. They are waiting. Waiting.

JEN: This sucks.

BETHANY: You always say that.

JEN: This always sucks.

BETHANY: You just need to adjust your expectations.

JEN: I don't think it's unreasonable to expect that the person who schedules these meetings would actually show up on time.

BETHANY: But she never does.

JEN: And, it sucks.

BETHANY: It could be worse.

JEN: That's how I should adjust my expectations? By thinking it could be worse?

BETHANY: Why not? Look. Elaine is late. And while she's late, I'm sitting here, happily chatting with my friend Jen and getting paid to do it. You, on the other hand, are all worked up over something that happens every single time we have our weekly meeting. Who's better off? Me. Why? Very low expectations.

JEN: Amazing.

BETHANY: You just need an attitude adjustment.

JEN: I need to have my attitude surgically removed.

(Elaine enters the room with her pile of meeting files.)

ELAINE: Good morning! Sorry I'm late.

BETHANY: No problem!

JEN: No problem.

ELAINE: So, how were your weekends?

BETHANY: SO great.

ELAINE: Great! Jen, how was yours?

JEN: Exhausting, short, awful.

ELAINE: *(Wasn't listening.)* Great.

BETHANY: Did you do anything fun?

ELAINE: Nope! So! Let's go ahead and get started.

BETHANY: *(Peeling an orange.)* Anybody want an orange? I have like twelve of them in my bag.

ELAINE: You know, before we begin, I should let you both know that I've asked Jack to join us for a few quick moments this morning.

JEN: *(Pause.)* Jack?

BETHANY: Sales Jack?

ELAINE: Well, of course sales Jack.

JEN: Sales Jack is coming here? Now?

BETHANY: But, this is our Monday morning meeting. OUR Monday morning meeting. I mean, this is supposed to be our safe place.

ELAINE: Well, you two brought up what I consider to be some very important issues last week, and I thought it would be beneficial for the four of us to begin a mutual dialogue.

BETHANY: But Elaine, we hate him.

ELAINE: Oh, you do not.

BETHANY: Oh, yes. We do.

JEN: You just need to adjust your expectations.

BETHANY: I did. I can't adjust any lower with him.

ELAINE: So, while we're waiting for Jack, let's look at what's on everybody's plate this week.

JEN: Wait, what are we supposed to say to Jack?

ELAINE: Whatever you think will help.

JEN: Help what?

ELAINE: The situation.

JEN: Elaine, I'm sorry, but the situation is that he's totally incompetent, he makes our jobs impossible, and he should be fired.

ELAINE: I don't think that will help the situation.

BETHANY: I don't care if he's incompetent. I just hate him.

ELAINE: But what's behind that?

BETHANY: Yesterday, I had this really important question? So I e-mailed him, and I left him about twelve voice mails, and he never called me back. Just totally ignored me. He always does that.

JEN: He does.

BETHANY: I mean, he's sales, and we're customer support, right, but he never tells us anything that's going on until suddenly somebody calls with this out-of-control problem, and they're like, "Oh, Jack said I should just call you." Hello, I don't know what's going on, I've never even heard of them before, and obviously, I look like a total idiot. Oh, and the way he always calls us his "girls" — I mean, I'm not a feminist or anything, but that totally bugs. "Just call my girls, they'll take care of you." God! He makes me want to, I don't know, throw things, or, or shoot somebody.

JEN: Awesome. *(Pause.)* Sorry.

ELAINE: Well. It seems that perhaps the core issue here is actually a simple personality conflict.

JEN: Um. I like him OK.

ELAINE: Great!

JEN: He doesn't mean to be insensitive. I think he has a good heart.

ELAINE: Yes, I think he does.

JEN: I just think he's utterly incompetent and should be fired.

BETHANY: Or shot. *(Oops — puts her hands over her mouth.)*

ELAINE: OK. Let's talk facts. Jack is the sales specialist for our region, agreed. We are his assigned customer support specialists, agreed. Clearly we need to be able to work as a team, together. Agreed? I'm not asking you to *like* Jack . . . I'm just asking you to treat him with the respect he deserves, as a person who is doing his best. Right? You said it yourself, he has a good heart. He's doing the best that he can.

(Bethany and Jen consider this. She's probably right.)

ELAINE: We are all doing the best that we can.

BETHANY: I will do my best to be nice to Jack.

JEN: But we still need to talk about the stuff you were saying. Elaine, you're the team leader . . . just, please be sure to bring that stuff up, OK?

ELAINE: Absolutely.

(Jack enters.)

JACK: Good morning, ladies!

ELAINE: Jack! Good morning. Thanks for stopping by.

BETHANY AND JEN: Hey.

JACK: No problem. So, what I miss?

ELAINE: Oh, nothing, really, we've just been chatting about our weekends.

JACK: And how were they?

BETHANY: SO great.

ELAINE: Thanks for asking.

JACK: Jen, how was yours?

JEN: Fabulous. Thanks.

JACK: Great.

ELAINE: *(Pause.)* So. Jack. We thought it would be helpful for the four of us to talk this morning about a few different issues that have come up.

JACK: You have some issues.

ELAINE: Well, not ISSUES, issues.

JACK: Great.

ELAINE: Great. So, Jack. I've asked you here today because the three of us would like to chat about what it is we can do to help make your job easier. That is to say, what could we do to help make you as effective as possible at what you do?

JACK: That's awfully nice.

ELAINE: We're all on the same team. Your team.

JACK: Right.

BETHANY: *(Pause.)* I think what we kind of want to know is, is there anything we could be doing to *partner* with you, with the customers. It just seems like maybe, I don't know, maybe we should be working more closely together.

JACK: I'm not sure I'm following.

(Bethany looks to Elaine for help. Elaine smiles blankly.)

BETHANY: Um, well. Like when a customer has a problem, do you think that, I don't know, maybe you could tell us what's going on, you know, before they call us?

JACK: Sure!

BETHANY: Oh. Great.

JACK: Anything else?

JEN: *(Giving it a try.)* Jack. I guess maybe we're feeling like we should be more closely involved with the sales process from the start. And that way we can be more familiar with the customers and the specific issues they're facing . . .

JACK: *(Interrupts Jen after "customers.")* You know, no offense meant here, but after nearly ten years in professional sales, I think I can handle my customers. I just don't think your department really understands what all is involved pre-sales, which is fine. That's why I'm in sales and you're in support, right? Sales is a multi-layered process that can't always be predicted or precisely measured. I really don't see where it is you feel you need to be "brought in."

BETHANY: But when you're working with the customers and they have a problem and you give them our number . . .

JACK: Exactly. It's great to know I can count on your team no matter what. Really, if I need anything, I'll let you know.

ELAINE: Perfect. Great.

JEN: I don't, um, I don't really feel like this exactly resolves what Bethany is getting at.

ELAINE: What else do you need to hear, Jen?

JEN: Well, Jack *(She's going to go for it.)* . . . do you like your job?

JACK: Sure. Sure, I like my job.

JEN: Because, well, we try really hard to help your customers, and well, I guess I don't see you trying very hard. At anything. Ever.

ELAINE: Now, Jen, let's not . . .

JEN: What I want to say here, Jack, is that what we don't, I don't really see in you is passion. For what you do.

JACK: I don't think passion was in my job description.

JEN: Well, obviously, but . . .

JACK: I sell telecommunications equipment to companies with two hundred and fifty employees or less. There's only so much to get excited about there.

ELAINE: Jack, Jen is certainly not questioning your commitment . . .

JEN: Let's take Bethany, here. Bethany is a customer support specialist for a telecommunications company. When people ask her what she does, and she tells them, they say, "That's great!" But they might be thinking, it would be within their rights to think, "Well, this person isn't exactly changing the world with that, now is she?" But the thing is, I think in Bethany's mind, she *is* changing something, doing some good for somebody. Let's say there's this one guy who's in, I don't know, Kenosha or something . . . this one guy is out there, trying his best daily to accomplish some stupid set of menial tasks, and every day he is absolutely counting on being able to pick up the phone that you sold him and knowing he can make a call. And one day, his phone, our phone, fails him. And that day, maybe Bethany talks to him, answers his questions, and fixes the problem. Now the phone works, and she's made one of the 10 million problems this guy has just because he's a human being go away. And knowing Bethany? She'll be grateful that she was given the opportunity to help.

That kind of thinking. That's passion. That's what makes Bethany a great person — no, a great woman — to work with. Commitment. Co-operation. Common courtesy. That's what we want from our team members.

(No one knows what to say. In the silence, Bethany chugs her entire Diet Coke and crushes the can with one hand.)

ELAINE: Jack, we're on your team.

JACK: Right.

ELAINE: Aren't we, girls?

JEN: That's it? "Girls"?

ELAINE: Thanks so much for coming by this morning, Jack.

JEN: We're not going to talk about this?

ELAINE: We just did, and it's late, and Jack needs to get going.

JACK: Thanks, Elaine.

JEN: Amazing. Absolutely amazing.

ELAINE: Jen, we can continue this conversation . . .

JEN: You know, we always talk, and ~~shit~~ *Stuff* always comes up, and everyone is nice, and no one ever says anything because we don't want anything to disrupt this illusion we have of forward movement. Which, what does that mean anyway? What exactly are we measuring to determine movement? Do you even know?

ELAINE: We're all done here.

JEN: We are not done.

ELAINE: We're done, I say we're done.

JEN: You know, Bethany is convinced that Jack is the problem because he's so clued out 98 percent of the time, but it's really you. It's the way you just smile and nod and say we're all doing our best, we're all on the same team, we all need to respect each other —

ELAINE: Jen, let's try to keep our emotions under control . . .

JEN: You say, "We need to be patient, we need to stick together," and then nothing ever changes because you're so worried about pissing somebody off, like somehow that would move us backward if there were tension or conflict or God *forbid* someone got angry . . .

ELAINE: You know, don't blame me because you're an unhappy person. I like my job here. I like coming in to a place every day where I know everyone is nice, and professional, and respectful, and we all like each other.

JEN: And nothing ever changes, does it, Elaine?

ELAINE: What is so wrong with things the way they are? Why does anything need to change? *Pitiful*

JEN: Oh, you're right. ~~Shitty~~ sales, ~~fucked-up~~ nonexistent communication, general mediocrity everywhere you turn, what's wrong with that?

ELAINE: Oh, and you are so much better than that.

JEN: No, Elaine, I'm not. ~~I'm shitty and~~ I'm mediocre. But I don't want to be. I want to be passionate. I want to be inspired. I want to know that what I do means something, that there is an effect, a shift, even a ~~goddamn~~ ripple . . .

ELAINE: But listen to me, Jen. As your team leader, I'm telling you, there is. You contribute. You make a difference. I'm telling you, you matter.

JEN: But I don't respect you.

(Stunned silence. Elaine musters what little remaining dignity she can, picks up her pile of files and legal pads, and walks out.)

JACK: Hey, 9:30 already? Whoa, time flies when you're having fun. So. I guess I'll just see you around. Jen? For what it's worth . . . I think you're doing a great job. *(Jack exits. Bethany and Jen sit together. Finally, Bethany gathers up her crap and simply exits. Jen sits at the table and begins to recite to herself, perhaps adding movement or volume as it builds.)*

JEN: I'm doing the best that I can. I'm doing the best that I can. I'm doing the best that I can. I'm doing the best that I can.

END OF PLAY

Fit for Feet

JORDAN HARRISON

Fit for Feet premiered at the Actors Theatre of Louisville,
Humana Festival 2003.

CHARACTERS

CLAIRE, late 20s. Nice sweater set. Pastels.

LINDA, 50s. Improbably blonde for her age.

JIMMY, late 20s. Average Joe in a baseball cap.

A PROMINENT DANCE CRITIC

PRODUCTION NOTE

This play is indebted to Joan Acocella's unexpurgated edition of Nijinsky's diaries.

FIT FOR FEET

Scene One

    Stage left. Linda and Claire in Adirondack chairs. Linda reclines, sipping an iced tea. Claire sits very straight, no iced tea.

LINDA: Isn't this civilized?

CLAIRE: It is the ultimate goal of civilization to sit and do nothing.
    (This silences Linda for a second.)

LINDA: How are my almost-newlyweds? How are my daughter and my wonderful new son?

CLAIRE: Jimmy thinks he's Nijinsky. The dancer. *(With added difficulty.)* Recently he's started to believe he's Nijinsky.
    (Stage right. Jimmy is sawing the heels off a pair of dress shoes. Claire can see him but Linda cannot.)

LINDA: Does he dance?

CLAIRE: Not well, so you wouldn't think —

LINDA: I adore dancing.

CLAIRE: That really isn't the issue.

LINDA: The ballet in particular. Old World beauty. Strong male legs. *Lifting.*

CLAIRE: Listen to me. I think he might be losing his mind. He thinks he's a dead Russian.

LINDA: Might he be right?

CLAIRE: Jimmy has never been to Russia. He sits at a desk every day. He is not a dancer.

LINDA: *(Airily.)* We should go to the ballet.
    (Stage right. Jimmy is finished with his sawing. He tries the shoes on. Success: Ballet slippers.)

LINDA: You might take a look at the seating chart. For the reception.
    (Pause. Claire has noticed Jimmy putting on the "slippers.")

LINDA: Mr. Barkley is at the same table as that Arkansas woman, and you know that won't do.
    (Claire gets out of her chair and crosses to Jimmy. He is doing pliés now, his back to her.)

LINDA: *(Calling after her.)* You might consider! *(Linda takes a resigned sip of iced tea. Her light fades.)*

CLAIRE: Can I ask what you're doing?

(*Jimmy stops cold, but doesn't turn around. We can see that there is music in his head.*)

JIMMY: My head's full of strange names. Diaghilev, Stravinsky, Ballet Russes. Romola, Kyra, Kostrovsky. But above all, Diaghilev. How I hate that diseased dog, and love him. As I love all God's creations. (*He begins a different exercise.*)

CLAIRE: Did anything happen recently, anything out of the ordinary?

(*He turns to her.*)

JIMMY: What is ordinary?

CLAIRE: Did you get hit on the head, did you cross a black cat, did you limbo a ladder?

JIMMY: There was the thing with the lightning.

CLAIRE: What with what?

JIMMY: I was walking along, minding my business —

CLAIRE: (*Gravely.*) That's how these things happen.

JIMMY: When out of the sky —

CLAIRE: Of course.

JIMMY: Would you mind not —

CLAIRE: Sorry.

JIMMY: Last Thursday. There hadn't been rain in the forecast, but I'm coming back from work — wouldn't you know, the sky is practically black. Jet black clouds, ions crashing in the air.

CLAIRE: Were you wearing your wedding shoes?

JIMMY: I figure I'll make it home in time if I take the shortcut through the field.

(*Claire's head in her hands.*)

JIMMY: On my way I see a cat up a tree, calico a few branches up. I start to climb, here kitty kitty, the storm all around me now. Then the Kaboom.

CLAIRE: You didn't tell me this last Thursday.

JIMMY: (*A sudden, regal change, evidenced in his posture.*) Thursday, Friday. All is the same in the great wheel of life.

CLAIRE: Why Nijinsky? That's what I don't get. Why not Nureyev, Baryshnikov, one of the other Kovs?

JIMMY: (*Speaking of himself in the third person.*) Nijinsky is the best.

CLAIRE: You're not the best.

JIMMY: Wait and see.

(*Stage left. Lights rise on Linda.*)

LINDA: You're hard on him, maybe that's it.

CLAIRE: I don't want there to be any illusions . . . *(Claire returns to her chair.)*

LINDA: Wait till you're married a year. Then you can turn shrew.

CLAIRE: . . . Any secrets. It's destructive.

LINDA: Letting that lady minister do your vows — *that's* destructive.

CLAIRE: We can still call the whole thing off.

(Linda removes a flask from her purse and pours something in her iced tea. She drinks deeply. Pause.)

LINDA: You left the iron on this morning.

CLAIRE: Oopsie.

LINDA: While you were dashing out.

CLAIRE: Good thing you saw it then.

(Stage right. Jimmy is drawing in a notebook with a crayon. Very heavily — the crayon is soon down to a stub.)

LINDA: Exactly, good thing. Or what would have happened, Claire. You might take a moment to consider.

(Claire doesn't take a moment.)

CLAIRE: The house would burn, the firemen would come, we arrive home to a charred black mess. You meet a kind fireman: Big hands, a good cook. I hear those men are always good cooks. And I won't have to look after you ever again. Jimmy and I go live in some foreign, sun-dappled place. Help me find some oily rags, some lighter fluid. We'll do it right now.

LINDA: You haven't considered at all.

CLAIRE: I'm kind of preoccupied.

LINDA: Consider. Think of Muffin, for starters.

(Sound of a yippy dog yipping. They look off stage and back, quickly.)

CLAIRE: We would grieve.

LINDA: The photographs. Everything your memory has come to rely on, melted down to a bubbling chemical ooze-thing.

CLAIRE: A person can't live in the past.

LINDA: The CLOTHES, Claire. You have beautiful clothes.

CLAIRE: Insurance, Mother —

LINDA: — Can't replace the chenille scarf.

CLAIRE: Milan.

LINDA: That poncho doohickey.

CLAIRE: It's a *caftan.* Johannesburg.

LINDA: Earrings.

CLAIRE: Antique Market, Copenhagen. *(With special pride.)* I haggled.

LINDA: Gorgeous.

CLAIRE: I thought so.

(Jimmy holds up his drawing, proudly, for the audience: many pairs of menacing eyes, peering out of darkness. Claire sees it and recoils.)

LINDA: Have you considered? The absolute destruction of all you've collected, all we've amassed that makes us us. All it takes is one everyday carelessness and POOF — what do you have, who ARE you now?

CLAIRE: I guess I hadn't considered.

(Blackout.)

Mini-Interlude

Jimmy performs a demented little solo here between the two scenes. He begins very awkwardly, but grows in confidence, until there is a vigorous assurance to his movements. (But he never ceases to be an average guy dancing ballet. Not Nijinsky.)

Scene Two

Claire and Linda in the Adirondack chairs, as before. They are examining Jimmy's drawing.

LINDA: Are those eyes?

CLAIRE: It's supposed to be soldiers, he told me.

LINDA: How creative.

CLAIRE: He's worse, I think. The other day I was all, "Darling, would you take a look at these china patterns?"

(Jimmy enters. He flings off his baseball cap, a romantic gesture — his hair smoothed off his forehead. Dapper. He acts out Claire's narrative.)

CLAIRE: He walked up to me, looking me in the eye the whole time, grabbed my wrist, said:

JIMMY: I am noise. I am youth. I am a great hammer.

CLAIRE: Normally if a guy said that to me, *especially* my husband, I'd be: "Yeah sure, you're a hammer. Now about these patterns." But he looks at me that new way and says:

JIMMY: I am a rebel angel, Romola. You are a lusterless moon. You are fit for my feet.

CLAIRE: And he holds me and calls me by that strange name and I am *happy* to be fit for his feet.

LINDA: Susan Faludi wouldn't approve, Claire.

CLAIRE: *(In his grip.)* There's more. We're still in this violent, like, erotic, like, *clench* and he says:

JIMMY: I am God in my prick. God is in me and I am in God.

CLAIRE: *(Catching her breath.)* Say that again?

JIMMY: I am in God.

CLAIRE: No, the other.

JIMMY: I am God in my prick.

CLAIRE: *(Pouncing on him.)* That's the one.

LINDA: You must be delighted.

CLAIRE: Delighted?

(Jimmy crawls out from under Claire and exits. She watches him leave.)

CLAIRE: It's true, I can't help but find him somewhat more . . . magnetic these days. This new confidence. Practicing jetés instead of scratching his pits.

LINDA: I'm not sure what you're complaining about.

CLAIRE: I don't *recognize* him. We're about to tell each other for better or for worse and I don't know who he is.

LINDA: Can we ever *know* a person, really? Why not be married to someone who wakes up different every morning? Every day a surprise.

CLAIRE: I chose *Jimmy*. That's what I want to wake up to. And maybe, every now and then, the virile and commanding Russian can come to visit.

LINDA: You were always the idealist, Claire.

CLAIRE: *(To herself.)* Maybe if I knew more about him.

LINDA: You've dated for it's been years.

CLAIRE: Nijinsky, I mean. If I did some research. Maybe this would make sense, if only we knew more.

(A Prominent Dance Critic enters. Haughty and urbane, she wears a dramatic, asymmetrical tunic. She reaches into the air and pulls down a white screen, center stage, without missing a beat. A slide of Nijinsky, in his famous Afternoon of a Faun *garb, appears.)*

CRITIC: Tragically, we lack a celluloid record of Nijinsky in performance. But we know from first-hand accounts — among them, that of his great countryman Vladimir Nabokov — that when he leapt in the air, he seemed to hover for a moment, as if suspended by a gold thread leading out of his brow and through the roof. Then, most remarkably, he lofted another inch before returning to Earth. Every evening, audiences at the Ballets Russes witnessed an assault on the principles of gravity the like of which we haven't seen — unassisted by coarse machinery — since the Newtonian apple grounded mankind's Icarian fancies.

CLAIRE: What can she mean?

LINDA: Guy jumped high in the sky.

CRITIC: Next slide, please.

(The slide changes to Nijinsky, looking quite mad now, in Stravinsky's Petrushka.)

CRITIC: But if Nijinsky's leap embodied that part of us that wants to leave this world behind, it was his mind that finally carried out the dare.

CLAIRE: Pardon?

CRITIC: He went positively bonkers. Abandoned by the ballet, the great man withdrew into the pages of his diary. Written on three notebooks in 1919, the diary evidences a mind in which sex and war, heaven and hell simmer in the same debauched stew. A rondo of rigmarole, penned in an uneasy blend of his native Russian, courtly French, childlike scribblings, and a sort of malignantly repetitive baby-talk. Gobbledy-gook driven by a cunningly transgressive illogic. Mother Goose gone prick-mad. Muttering, proselytizing, scatologically obsessed, biting the heads off crayons, Nijinsky had become as much an animal as a God. Is this the cost of genius? we ask the spheres. We are still deciphering the music of their answer.

(The Critic curtsies deeply. Her light is extinguished. The screen flies away.)

LINDA: My head hurts.

CLAIRE: It will soon hurt more. Last night, he climbed out of bed, sleepwalking, he does that.

(Jimmy crosses, his arms stretched out, somnambulist-style.)

CLAIRE: But never like this, all the way downstairs and out the front door. I put on a raincoat and followed him.

LINDA: A raincoat? With all your beautiful things . . .

CLAIRE: The most worrisome thing was he didn't trip once. Used to be he couldn't walk for his own shoelaces. Here he was, a bounce in his step,
Sidestepping cracks, sashaying past puddles, softly snoring all the time.
Soon we're in a part of town I've never been to.
Cobblestones, steaming potholes. Can those be gaslights?
I can't even catch sight of a Starbucks.
He seems to be practicing steps.
His arms striking the air, his legs like scissors.
As I watch him, I can almost hear the music he's dancing to,
And it's like he's lighter on his feet with every step.
People notice. All the motleys out at 3 AM:
Insomniacs with dark rings, child molesters, women with frosted hair.

(Linda gasps.)

CLAIRE: They all come out of the shadows and follow him,
They don't know why. How can they not?
Soon it's a little parade of freaks, with Jimmy at the head like a drum major.

And then he takes off.

(Stage right. Jimmy leaps into the air, hovers there, and lofts another inch before landing. Claire's hand at her mouth.)

CLAIRE: I'm peeking from behind a dumpster in my old raincoat,

My hair flat around my shoulders like a wet rat.

And I don't have anything to do with that brilliant thing in the air.

And he has even less to do with Jimmy.

Enough. I break the spell, I shake him awake.

He feels small in my arms, all the people watching us.

Then his eyes open on me, ash-black, and he says, "You try to keep me . . ."

JIMMY: *(Overlapping.)* You try to keep me down with the scalyskins and the black-eyed beasts but you are death. I am life and you are death.

LINDA: One should never wake people in the middle of dreams.

CLAIRE: Tomorrow we walk down the aisle and I'm *death*?

(Stage left. Linda touches Claire on the knee.)

LINDA: I'll have a talk with him, lamb.

(Stage right. Jimmy sits at a vanity, applying thick white pancake makeup. He is not effeminate about it. Rather it is a solemn ritual — putting on warpaint. Linda crosses to him.)

LINDA: Can you believe, the big day? Wait till you see Claire, like some kind of delicious, multi-leveled parfait. All that organza —

(Jimmy turns to her, face shocking-white.)

LINDA: Oh. *(Pause.)* Tell me my daughter's being a nervous bride. Tell me there's nothing the matter with our fine young management consultant.

JIMMY: *Je ne parle pas Anglais.*

(Stage left. Claire putting on her wedding dress. Nervous.)

LINDA: You just have to parle enough to say "I do."

JIMMY: *Je ne parle pas Anglais.*

LINDA: We don't have a lot of time. Where's your tux?

JIMMY: *Je ne parle de plus Anglais.*

LINDA: *(Trying another tack.) Je m'appelle Linda.* That's all I remember from high school, can you believe?

JIMMY: *(Rising.) Je suis boeff mes pas biffstek.*

LINDA: *Ça va bien, merci.* I'm afraid that's it, my whole bag of tricks.

JIMMY: *(Very close to her, a forceful whisper.)*

Je ne suis pas biffstek.

Je suis stek sans boeuf en biff.

LINDA: Oh my my my. *Ou est la Tour Eiffel?*

JIMMY: *(Slapping his thighs percussively with each "si.")*

Je ne suis je un tamboure.

Je suis si si si si si si si

LINDA: *(Smoldering now.)* Un pain au chocolat, s'il vous plait!

(Jimmy is elsewhere, oblivious to the game.)

JIMMY:

Tzi tzi tzi tzi tzi tzi tzi tzi

Je suis ça suis ça suis ça je ça

ça ça ça ça ça ça ça ça ça

LINDA: I'm afraid I lost track.

JIMMY: I am a lullabyer, I am a singer of all songs!

LINDA: *(Mischievously.)* I thought you didn't parle Anglais, Frenchie.

(Jimmy jumps. This time he does not come down. Linda looks up at him in awe, mouth ajar. There is music in her head. Claire stomps over, in full wedding dress.)

LINDA: Excellent young man!

CLAIRE: Come down come DOWN. *(Claire jumps after Jimmy, her arms flailing for him. After some failed attempts, she starts to take running leaps. Not even close. She continues to jump, more and more wildly. Sound of the "Wedding March" beginning. Quick blackout on Claire jumping into the air, her dress billowing around her.)*

END OF PLAY

Always

JON JORY

ALWAYS

A living space. Two young couples, one at the beginning of a relationship and one at the end. The point, of course, is that they are the same couple.

JOE 1: You are so beautiful, it drives me crazy.

ELLEN 1: And you, Joseph, are nearsighted which is why I picked you.

JOE 1: I can't believe you were attracted to me.

ELLEN 2: Joe?

ELLEN 1: Ah, we're fishing for compliments are we?

ELLEN 2: Your sister called.

JOE 1: Tell me the first moment you were attracted to me?

JOE 2: *(Entering.)* Ginny or Babs?

ELLEN 1: When I realized you couldn't do a crossword puzzle.

ELLEN 2: Ginny. She wants to know what the hell is wrong with us?

JOE 1: You were attracted because of my limited mental facility?

JOE 2: And you doubtless told her?

ELLEN 2: I told her what was wrong with us is what's wrong with you.

ELLEN 1: Because you were undefended and touching.

JOE 1: Thanks.

JOE 2: Thanks.

ELLEN 1: It wasn't a persona, it was a real quality.

JOE 2: Another case of you bad-mouthing me to my family.

JOE 1: And attraction number two?

ELLEN 2: No Joe. You treat me like dirt in public. You steal my spare change. You mess with my girlfriends. You tell me I'm worthless and fat. I'm not lying to your sister.

ELLEN 1: You're smart, you have wonderful hands, you don't put up with my crap and you buy me Sweet Mesquite Pringles.

JOE 2: Thanks for the list. My stuff's in the car.

ELLEN 2: You don't want a relationship . . .

JOE 2: Enough.

ELLEN 2: You want sex, food and a maid service.

JOE 2: Here's my parents' address if you need to send bills.

ELLEN 2: Really, you plan to start paying your bills?

JOE 1: Can we make a date so you can say those same things about me in a year.

JOE 2: I lost my job Ellen, as well you know.

ELLEN 1: I will say the same things in ten years.

ELLEN 2: Because you sexually harassed your fellow employees.

JOE 2: Hey. She was crazy, the charge was dismissed, they fired her.

ELLEN 1: So, Kiss me.

ELLEN 2: Don't touch me.

JOE 1: In the parking lot when I was getting groceries

JOE 2: I actually see couples walking around happy . . .

JOE 1: This couple was screaming at each other while she stood there nursing a baby.

JOE 2: I wanted to tell them to hit fast forward.

JOE 1: And I felt smug because it could never happen to us.

JOE 2: We were unbelievably naive.

JOE 1: We wouldn't let it happen.

JOE 2: Maybe all beginnings are naive.

ELLEN 1: No.

ELLEN 2: No.

JOE 1: Ellen, I have something for you.

JOE 2: There's something we haven't talked about.

ELLEN 1: Oh God . . .

JOE 2: Then I'll be out of here.

ELLEN 2: What?

JOE 1: OK . . . I bought you a ring.

JOE 2: I'm going to need the ring back.

ELLEN 1: I've been terrified you would do that.

ELLEN 2: Absolutely not.

ELLEN 1: Joe, it would be so formal. It would be so stiff and settled.

ELLEN 2: The person who gave me that ring is the person I want to remember.

ELLEN 1: I'm afraid to be a fact.

ELLEN 2: I want to remember what was possible.

JOE 1: You are a fact to me. Unchangeable.

JOE 2: The fact is, Ellen, I have to have the money.

ELLEN 1: You're so sure we won't screw this up?

JOE 2: I'm sorry.

JOE 1: I am.

ELLEN 1: I won't find out you're somebody else? You won't find out I am?

ELLEN 2: We were somebody else once. I don't even know who those people were.

JOE 1: Popeye the sailor man. I yam what I yam.

ELLEN 1: So the promise is that what I see is what I get?

JOE 2: You're the one who changed.

ELLEN 2: No I didn't, I woke up.

ELLEN 1: Tell me what this is?

JOE 1: It's what the miners call the bedrock. The stuff underneath the gravel.

ELLEN 1: I think I would like you to hand me that ring.

ELLEN 2: Here, take it. *(She holds it out.)*

JOE 1: With heart attached. *(He holds it out.)*

JOE 2: Thank you. Sorry it was temporary. See, people are all chaos. They're all flux. We never exist as something complete and trustworthy.

ELLEN 1: I just have to believe you know me and I know you. I guess more importantly I have to believe we know ourselves. We do right?

JOE 2: Maybe it has something to do with flow, with being 90 percent water. Anyway, I meant every damn thing I said when I gave it to you.

ELLEN 1: You mean this, right? There isn't any part of you in conflict with doing this? If there is tell me. Tell me and I won't take it.

JOE 2: And now I have to have it back. Those two things aren't in conflict. They just exist in two different parts of the river.

ELLEN 1: Because once I take this, that's it for me. I'll give over completely Joe. From then on there are no more decisions for me to make.

JOE 1: Believe me, I hear you.

ELLEN 2: I hear you. *(Ellen 1 and Joe 2 take the rings simultaneously.)*

ELLEN 1: Thank you.

JOE 2: Thank you.

ELLEN 2: What happens now?

JOE 1: What happens now?

JOE 2: The end.

ELLEN 1: Maybe just pizza.

ELLEN 2: I could use a pizza.

JOE 1: Pizza's good.

JOE 2: Pizza's good.

ELLEN 2: Pizza then.

JOE 2: I loved you.

JOE 1: I love you.

ELLEN 2: I loved you.

ELLEN 1: I love you. *(Ellen 1 and Joe 1 embrace.)*

JOE 2: I'll order.

JOE 1: I'll order.

JOE 2: You want the pepperoni under the cheese right?

ELLEN 2: On top.

JOE 2: You always said under.

ELLEN 2: No Joe.

ELLEN 1: Hey Joseph, tell them I like the pepperoni on top of the cheese.

JOE 1: You are incredibly retro.

ELLEN 1: Don't forget.

JOE 1: There's nothing about you I could forget.

ELLEN 2: You don't seem to remember anything about me from day to day.

JOE 2: Look, I'm just going to go.

ELLEN 2: Because you didn't remember?

JOE 2: Yeah.

JOE 1: So, pizza time.

ELLEN 1: You'll come right back.

ELLEN 2: Wrap it up. Cut the losses. Don't look back.

JOE 2: Pretty much.

ELLEN 2: Bye Joe.

JOE 1: Back in a flash.

JOE 2: Maybe down the road.

ELLEN 2: No Joe.

ELLEN 1: Now and forever.

(The men leave. The women sit. Blackout.)

END OF PLAY

No More Static

KEVIN KELL O'DONNELL

No More Static was commisioned by
and premiered at the Guthrie Theater,
Joe Dowling, Artistic Director.

CHARACTERS

LIAM, 26, Irish-American.
SCOTT, 27, African-American.
LEX, 26, American.
NORA, 20, Liam's sister.

SETTING

Riverside Park, New York City, under the George Washington Bridge, next to the Little Red Lighthouse. There's a concrete path, a bench next to the Lighthouse, green grass, and not a cloud in the sky.

TIME

Late Spring, 2003.

SPECIAL NOTE

The Little Red Lighthouse can be represented with lighting. It isn't necessary to have an actual lighthouse.

NO MORE STATIC

Liam, Scott and Lex look out over a rail at the Hudson River. Lex is dressed in a disheveled spring polyester suit. Scott is dressed in sweat pants, sandals, and a T-shirt. He plays with a yo-yo. Liam wears jeans, a spring jacket, and a Boston Red Sox baseball cap. He has a cut under his left eye.

LIAM: How do you guys do it?

LEX: What?

LIAM: Live here with all the shit going on?

SCOTT: With lots of money.

LEX: Maybe for you, rock star.

SCOTT: No, seriously, it does get crazy here. Sometimes you forget about the insanity, sometimes you embrace it.

LIAM: You take vacations? Get away?

LEX: Who the fuck can afford vacations? I went home for Christmas. Depressed the shit out of me.

LIAM: What're you talking about, you weren't depressed when I came and saw you — you were happy —

LEX: I was drunk.

LIAM: Well, it was Christmas, 'course you were. *(Pause.)* I'm glad we came here. It's not part of the rest of this place. Jesus, look at that house, you see that over there? It's like a little cabin — little beach. Might be a boat.

LEX: Oh, Yeah.

LIAM: It's just out of place, you know? Like this fuckin' lighthouse. That's New Jersey, right?

(Lex and Scott laugh.)

LEX: It's kind of cool to be with you down here. If you moved down, Jesus, that'd be great. The three of us reunited in the big city.

SCOTT: I feel like I'm taking my kid to school for the first time. I can't help thinking, *he'll never be this innocent again.*

LIAM: Stop busting my balls.

SCOTT: Sorry, dude, but it's true.

LEX: Seriously, maybe you should think about moving down here Lee.

LIAM: Nah. There's lots of stuff going on back home right now.

LEX: Like what?

LIAM: I got work, you know.

SCOTT: You could find something down here.

LEX: Maybe flipping burgers somewhere. It's just this economy . . .

SCOTT: Hence, your endless job search.

LIAM: I'm trying to pay off the house. It's where I'm supposed to be right now.

LEX: How's that going, by the way?

LIAM: It's fine. I'm really close. I got a few projects — finishing a walkway down on Jerusalem Road, and another spring cleanup scheduled. I should be all right.

LEX: That's great, man. After you pay off the joint, then you can move down here, huh? *(Liam shrugs.)* It's just a thought. But you know, it's nice to think you're still back there, keeping it safe. This city, it's not good enough for you anyway, brotha.

LIAM: Thanks, dude. Hey, Scott? So, this show tomorrow, are we gonna have to dress up, 'cause I didn't bring anything fancy, you know? I'm not like Dapper Dan over here.

SCOTT: No, don't worry about it. It's an opening, you only dress up if you don't know the artist.

LIAM: Good to know. Hey, I'll be right back.

LEX: Where are you going?

LIAM: I want to touch the water.

SCOTT: It's not really clean, you know?

LIAM: I'll be right back. *(He leaves.)*

SCOTT: Lee, seriously, it's like, dangerous.

LEX: Do you think this is a good idea?

SCOTT: I know this is what she wants.

LEX: I just hope he doesn't freak out when she shows up.

SCOTT: Why would he?

LEX: 'Cause of the thing.

SCOTT: What thing?

LEX: The money.

SCOTT: What?

LEX: I thought you — she stole about three grand from the kid before she took off. Drew it right out of the account, a week after their mother died. I thought you knew about that.

SCOTT: I didn't know about her stealing money. What did he do?

LEX: It's his sister. I mean, what's he going to do? Besides, she hasn't told him where she is. He told me he gets letters from her, but she doesn't say where she is. Postmarked all over the place.

SCOTT: She told me she's been living here for a few months. Bartending.

LEX: The kid's had enough tragedy in his life this year. I just don't want him to get hurt. I'm only here to protect him. I'm not concerned about her. You know he's still not over his mom.

SCOTT: Of course he isn't.

LEX: And do you remember Jenny?

SCOTT: I met her at the funeral. That was the only time. She was nice.

LEX: Dude, she was perfect. Great girl. And she loved the kid. But, she only knew him sober. When Nora left him and took all that money, the kid started playing pharmacist with himself. Must have scared the shit out of his girl. He called me one night, back in November, crying. She left a note for him. Liam told me he would never forgive Nora. He blamed her. If she hadn't left, he wouldn't have started drinking again.

SCOTT: He blamed Nora for that?

LEX: Why do you have to be so — YES he blamed her. What? You can't understand that?

SCOTT: Look, do you think he's still mad at her?

LEX: I don't know. Pretty damn good chance.

SCOTT: Do you know he hit her?

LEX: What?

SCOTT: She came home late, he was drunk — waiting up for her. Something about her boyfriend. He didn't like the guy. That's why Nora took off, Lex. He cut her cheek open.

LEX: Goddamnit Liam.

SCOTT: And do you know he spent some time in jail?

LEX: Jail?

SCOTT: For a week in January. He was at Mo Jo's. Jenny walked in with some guy. Liam ended up cracking the guy's head open on a radiator. Nora said they held him for a week, but the guy ended up not pressing charges. The kid's in trouble. Look at his face — you really believe that's a carpentry accident?

LEX: Damn, I hope we're doing the right thing. *(Pause.)* We really haven't thought this through man — I mean, if he hit her then —

SCOTT: I think she wants to make peace with him about it.

LEX: She say that?

SCOTT: No but —

LEX: See, he should just move down here with us. We'll take care of him.

SCOTT: I know. I want that too. But it's his call.

LEX: I just miss him, you know. You find out real quick who you want to be around when you lose your . . . way. When I got laid off, and then when Sarah left, I thought about him a lot: up there in Boston, working, writing when he could. But I had a feeling something was wrong. Couldn't call him — his phone was turned off.

SCOTT: Yeah, I know.

LEX: No computer. Nothing. I wrote him a letter, but I felt stupid about it. I just kept going on and on about the old days, and — well, you know me. I kept it though.

SCOTT: You should give it to him.

LEX: We'll see. I need a drink. *(Pulls out a flask from his jacket and takes a swig.)*
(Scott's cell phone rings.)

SCOTT: Hello? Yeah. Hi, yeah we're here. Yup, he's *(Looks around, can't see Liam.)* around. I mean, he's here. All right. All right. Well, the park is going to close at six. Sundown. Yeah. So if you want — shit.

LEX: What?

SCOTT: The fuckin' phone went out.

LEX: It's because you're under the bridge. Move over here.
(Scott moves and redials the phone.)

SCOTT: Wouldn't the bridge help the signal?

LEX: Help the signal?

SCOTT: Yeah, since it's so high — Hello? Nora? It's Scott. Sorry about that. I said I'm sorry about that. I'M SORRY ABOUT THAT. Oh, sorry. So anyway. We're here, by the lighthouse and we'll stay here until you come, or somebody kicks us out. Where are you right now? Really. Damn. Well, just hang in there — Ahh! JESUS CHRIST!!! My fucking ear!

LEX: What the hell's wrong?
(Scott is holding his hand up to his ear. He's doubled over in pain.)

SCOTT: This static just went through the phone. It was like a lightning bolt. Jesus.

LEX: So where is she?

SCOTT: She's at One Twenty Five. Train's stopped.

LEX: She's not going to make it. Just as well.

SCOTT: She will.

LEX: Why does she want to meet him here anyway?

SCOTT: I don't know. When she told me, I didn't know where she meant,
(Lex begins reading the plaque on the ground next to the lighthouse.)

SCOTT: and she was like, "You know the Little Red Lighthouse from the book," I was like, "No, sorry I don't know."

LEX: Yeah, they made it into a book. Look: "Immortalized in the children's book *The Little Red Lighthouse and the Great Gray Bridge (Lex looks up at the George Washington Bridge.)* by Hildegarde H. Swift published in 1942. In the book the lighthouse learns that it still has an important job to do, and that there is still a place in the world for an old lighthouse."

SCOTT: Signed Rudolph Giuliani. Do you think he really wrote that?

LEX: How the hell should I know?

SCOTT: What's the matter with you?

LEX: Nothing. I'm just curious why she wants to meet him here, and you're cracking jokes.

SCOTT: Jokes?

LEX: Yeah, everything's always so cool with you isn't it?

SCOTT: What the hell are you talking about?

LEX: Nothing.

SCOTT: Nothing? Fine.

LEX: Yeah, fine.

SCOTT: Lex, what's going on?

LEX: I said: nothing.

SCOTT: You got something to say to me why don't you say it and stop acting like a bitch.

LEX: You're so . . .

SCOTT: What?

LEX: That piece you're working on right now . . . It's really great, dude. I can't tell you why. But, I just know it's really . . . different from your other stuff . . . and your other stuff is incredible . . . but, even with all this, the stuff that's been happening to you — your success — you're still going. You're still improving.

SCOTT: It's what I do.

LEX: I know.

SCOTT: You're good at what you do.

LEX: Don't fuck with me.

SCOTT: I'm serious. I couldn't do that type of work. Numbers, money. I'd be lost.

LEX: Do you remember in college, when I was thinking of asking Sarah to marry me? Do you remember what you said to me?

SCOTT: No.

LEX: You asked me what my dreams were. What I wanted to do before I died. We sat down and made a list of things we wanted to do before we died. Like jump out of an airplane.

SCOTT: Visit the pyramids.

LEX: Have sex with two women.

SCOTT: Check.

LEX: Shut the fuck up.

SCOTT: Seriously.

LEX: When?

SCOTT: First year I came down.

LEX: You lucky son of a bitch.

SCOTT: What else?

LEX: Direct a movie.

SCOTT: Who said that?

LEX: I did. I said that.

    (Liam comes back over to them. He sees Lex with the flask.)

LIAM: Gimme some of that.

LEX: Ah, sure. *(He reluctantly gives him the flask.)*

LIAM: *(Takes a swig.)* You were right, the water was fuckin' disgusting. You guys
    ready to take off?

SCOTT: Let's hang out for a little longer, all right?

LIAM: Sure. It's the nicest place we've been so far.

LEX: You really couldn't see yourself down here?

LIAM: If I did move down here, it'd be for you guys. I love you guys, but I
    just — I have to finish things.

SCOTT: What do you mean?

LIAM: Well, the house. My parents came over here with nothin' at all, and now
    I have a chance to do something, to finish something up there.

LEX: But don't you think —

LIAM: And then there's Nora. I don't know where she is, but I know she'll be
    back.

SCOTT: When was the last time you heard from her?

LIAM: She wrote me a letter — said she was bartending in New Mexico. Before
    that, she was in California. My father used to call her his little sparrow.
    She always wanted to fly to the next thing.

LEX: She may not want to come back to you, Lee. You ever think of that?

SCOTT: Maybe she's happy wherever she is.

LIAM: How the fuck do you know she's happy?

SCOTT: I'm just saying.

LIAM: Exactly, you're just saying.

LEX: Lee, take it easy.

LIAM: I don't know if she's alive or not day to day and you guys don't know shit
    about that.

LEX: Look, we're down here . . .

SCOTT: She may not come back —

LIAM: So you're saying I should just close up shop and find a nice little studio apartment down here? I can't just be like you, Scott. I can't just come down here and paint pictures and float through. I've got responsibilities.

(Nora appears behind Liam. Lex and Scott immediately notice her.)

LIAM: I've got to make sure that she has a place that she can come back to when she chooses to come back — which she will. And it's not about me, it's not about how I feel about her, it's what I have to do. And Lex, I can't be like you either. If I get laid off from a job, I'm going to find another job. And you know what: fuck Sarah, all right. Stop using that as an excuse . . . I can't just come down here and live some childhood dream or something or live some New York fantasy. This city is terrible. It sucks. The place is dirty, it's expensive, it smells, and it's a huge target. Everybody goes around paranoid. Christ, I've only been here for two days, and I'm paranoid. Why would I want to come down and live here? It'd be like living on a big, gray bomb.

LEX: Look behind you, brotha.

(Liam turns around and sees Nora. After a moment, Lex and Scott back away, giving them their space. Liam at first doesn't recognize her. But when she starts walking toward him he gasps in disbelief. She embraces him, but he hardly responds. After a moment, she releases him. She then takes out an envelope and puts it in his hand. A moment passes. Liam opens the envelope. He takes out a letter and a check. He looks at the check. He then reads the letter to himself. He looks up and slowly turns around and looks at the Little Red Lighthouse. He looks back at the letter, then back at Nora. He gives the check back to Nora. She takes it. He takes her head in his hands and kisses her cheek. They embrace. She slips the check into the back pocket of his jeans. Blackout.)

END OF PLAY

PLAYS FOR
FIVE ACTORS

The Second Beam

JOAN ACKERMANN

The Second Beam was commissioned by
and premiered at the Guthrie Theater,
Joe Dowling, Artistic Director.

THE SECOND BEAM

In a waiting room with two doors for exits, three women — Georgia, Jennifer and Meg, all dressed in various ways as scientists for an audition — sit still on folding chairs and study four pages of sides (pages with lines for scenes). After a moment, a woman, a casting agent, opens one of the door and sticks her head in.

CASTING AGENT: Georgia?
　　(Georgia smiles up at her, grabs her stuff and exits. They smile at her and she exits into the audition room, closing the door behind her. Meg is the older of the two, more mature, grounded. Jennifer is soft-spoken, sweet.)
JENNIFER: Pardon me . . . Do you have a tissue?
　　(Meg opens her bag and gives her one. Goes back to her sides. Jennifer takes the tissue and wipes under both her armpits, discreetly but efficiently.)
JENNIFER: You were at *The Flannerys.*
　　(Meg looks at her blankly.)
JENNIFER: You read for the sister. Of the boxer, with the bad hand. The malpractice suit.
MEG: *(Remembering.)* Oh. Right.
JENNIFER: I heard that show didn't get picked up. *(Pause.)* You were at *Mind of a Married Man,* too. The jockey's wife. Are you memorizing that?
MEG: *(Friendly.)* No. No, just studying. *(Pause.)*
JENNIFER: Do you happen to know who got the part?
MEG: Which part. The sister, of the boxer?
JENNIFER: No. Yes.
MEG: Or the jockey's wife.
JENNIFER: Either. Both.
MEG: Well, the same actress got them both.
JENNIFER: Patti Scharer?
MEG: Patti Scharer.
JENNIFER: I knew it. Patti Scharer. Fucking Patti Scharer, pardon me. Every part my agent sends me out on, every single part it seems, Patti Scharer gets. Care for a mint?
　　(Meg shakes her head no, takes out a lipstick and puts some on, looking at herself in a small compact mirror.)
JENNIFER: Are you doing an accent?

MEG: Accent?

JENNIFER: For the scientist.

MEG: What kind of accent?

JENNIFER: Foreign.

MEG: I think she's American.

> *(Pause.)*

JENNIFER: So you're not doing an accent?

> *(Meg shakes her head, picks up the sides.)*

JENNIFER: I was going to do a French accent. Madame Curie. The scientist. You don't think I should?

MEG: If you've worked on it that way. It's a choice.

JENNIFER: Yes, it is. It's a choice. *(Pause.)* I never know about choices. My agent always says they like it when you make a choice, but I'm not so sure. I've been making choices, strong choices, but . . . they haven't really been panning out for me. *(She discreetly picks something out from between her teeth.)* I really need the work. I really, really, really need the work. I'm sorry, I'll let you concentrate. *(Pause.)* Have you read for him before?

> *(Meg looks at her.)*

JENNIFER: Ethan Schroeder. The director. Have you read for him?

> *(Meg nods, goes back to studying.)*

JENNIFER: My friend Annette says he's a monster. She read for him for a movie of the week and he ate his lunch the entire time.

MEG: He can be a jerk.

JENNIFER: That's all I need. *(She sighs, smooths her skirt.)* Can I just ask you . . . is this lipstick, the color of my lipstick, all right? I've never worn this shade before.

MEG: It looks good on you. It's a good color for you.

JENNIFER: You think so? Really?

MEG: I do. *(Smiling.)* It's a good choice.

JENNIFER: Thanks. I don't know. It felt like a scientist choice, I don't know why. Sometimes you just have to go with your gut.

> *(Meg nods. Jennifer, legs crossed, bobs a foot up and down.)*

JENNIFER: Patti Scharer. Do you get the light thing? They won't expect us to understand that, do you think? Stopping light? They won't grill us about that.

MEG: Probably not.

JENNIFER: I don't know. I read for the part of a veterinarian and they acted like they expected me to know everything about a dog's digestive system. I just winged it, talked about heartworm. I've seen them. In a jar. *(Jennifer grimaces slightly at the memory of them. Looks around. Pause.)* It's not just about the money. Truth be known, I'm feeling kind of stuck. *(Pause.)* If he's eating in there, if he's eating, stuffing his mouth with California pizza, Koo-koo Charoo chicken . . . You said you've read for him?

MEG: I used to go out with him.

JENNIFER: *(Stunned.)* You went out with him? You went out with Ethan Shroeder?

(Meg nods.)

JENNIFER: Ohmygod, I'm so sorry. What I said . . . I didn't mean to call him a monster. Maybe he was just . . . hungry when my friend read for him. Maybe he's perfectly . . .

MEG: It's OK. A lot of people think he's an asshole.

JENNIFER: They do. You're not going out with him anymore?

(Meg shakes her head.)

JENNIFER: You're still friends? I mean, you're OK reading for him?

MEG: I really like this part.

JENNIFER: You do?

MEG: I do. How often does that happen?

JENNIFER: Yeah. Really. *(Pause.)* You must like this part.

MEG: I find the subject fascinating. I've read quite a bit about it.

JENNIFER: Oh. So . . . Light travels a hundred and eighty thousand miles an hour . . .

MEG: A second.

JENNIFER: And . . . *(Jennifer waits for Meg to explain it.)* Then they stop it in a jar. *(Smiling.)* Like heartworm. Preserve it in formaldehyde.

MEG: Chilled sodium gas, actually.

JENNIFER: It just hangs in there? Frozen?

MEG: Well, the light goes out. It gets fainter and fainter as it slows down. The most amazing part, to me — it's all amazing — they can revive the light anytime by flashing a second beam of light through the gas.

JENNIFER: Oh.

MEG: They can bring a beam of light to a full stop, hold it, and then send it on its way with a second beam.

(Pause.)

JENNIFER: I like scenes best . . . when I can go deep. Cry. I like emotion. My background is theater.

MEG: Not a lot of emotion in these scenes, not ostensibly.

JENNIFER: No. That's why I was thinking the French . . .

MEG: Go for the accent.

JENNIFER: You think so?

> *(Another actress enters. She is very appealing, made-up, a knockout. She takes a seat. Exudes confidence. Both Meg and Jennifer look at her, silently, as she takes out six pages and starts going through them.)*

PATTI: *(To Jennifer, all business.)* Excuse me, are your pages with the reporter dated May eleventh or May fifteenth?

> *(Jennifer looks at her pages, confused, looks at Patti . . .)*

JENNIFER: The reporter? I don't have . . .

PATTI: Never mind. *Meg.*

MEG: Hi, Patti.

PATTI: How *are* you?

> *(Meg nods, friendly, a little guarded.)*

PATTI: It's so great to see you, are you here now?

MEG: I'm here.

PATTI: You know I'd heard that. I ran into Carolyn, she's stage managing *Vanya* at the Taper, she told me you'd moved back.

MEG: I did.

PATTI: That's great. And you're reading for Ethan?

MEG: I am.

PATTI: Wow. Wow. *(Patti waits for some kind of response from Meg who is not forthcoming.)*

MEG: How's Olivia?

PATTI: Olivia is three, God help me. Meg, can I borrow your lipstick, I actually forgot mine.

MEG: I'm sorry. I actually left all my makeup in my car.

PATTI: Really? What were you thinking?

> *(Patti maintains her charming smile as she studies Meg. Jennifer is staring at Patti in a mixed stupor of defeat and envy.)*

JENNIFER: *(Stirring.)* I have some lipstick. You can borrow.

PATTI: *(Brightly.)* Great. Thanks.

> *(Jennifer reaches down into her purse and takes out her lipstick, takes off the cap, and offers it to Patti.)*

PATTI: *(Looking at Jennifer's lips.)* Oh. Is it the color you're wearing?

JENNIFER: Uh-huh.

PATTI: That's OK. That color . . . I can't wear that color. But, thanks.

> *(Mortified, Jennifer looks down at the color, gradually retreats her hand, puts the cover back on and sticks the lipstick back in her purse. Pause as all study their sides.)*

PATTI: *(To Meg.)* I admire you, Meg. I really do. Reading for Ethan. That takes guts.

MEG: Not really.

PATTI: The way he treated you. You know Carolyn's First AD.

(Meg nods.)

PATTI: You know they're an item. Ethan and Carolyn. She's pregnant. That's ironic, huh?

(Meg did not know this. She flinches slightly. The door opens and Georgia enters with the casting agent behind her. Georgia grabs a sweater she left on a chair, waves to the casting agent, exiting.)

CASTING AGENT: Thanks, Georgia. Patti. You made it.

PATTI: I'm so sorry I'm late. The 405 was a nightmare.

CASTING AGENT: You want to come in? Or do you want to take a minute. Jennifer . . . ?

(Jennifer, discombobulated, jumps up, dropping all her pages as Patti grabs her purse, coat, stands up.)

PATTI: I'm fine. *(Patti heads into the audition room. The casting agent smiles at Meg and Jennifer . . . The casting agent exits into the audition room, closing the door behind her. Silence.)*

JENNIFER: *(Quietly.)* I'm sorry. Do you have another tissue?

(Meg hands her another tissue which Jennifer uses to wipe away a few tears before taking the lipstick out of her purse and dropping it into a trashcan. She grabs her stuff and stands, heads for the door going out.)

JENNIFER: It was very nice meeting you.

MEG: Where are you going?

JENNIFER: *(Sniffling, crying.)* I don't know. Bye.

MEG: Wait!

(Jennifer turns and looks at her.)

MEG: You can get this part.

JENNIFER: I can't get this part.

MEG: You can.

JENNIFER: I can't. I can't even audition for this part.

MEG: Sit down.

JENNIFER: What?

MEG: Pull yourself together. Sit down.

JENNIFER: *(Crying. Discombobulated.)* Where?

MEG: On that chair. Go ahead.

(Jennifer sits back down on her chair, sniffling.)

MEG: Here. Put these on. *(Meg takes a pair of tortoiseshell glasses out of her purse and gives them to Jennifer.)* Put them on.

JENNIFER: Why does she want this part? It's not even very big.

(Jennifer does.)

MEG: Patti Scharer is not going to get this part.

JENNIFER: Yes, she is.

MEG: No, she's not.

JENNIFER: *(Crying.)* She's already got it. She's already in there, with the part.

MEG: Ethan can't stand Patti Scharer. He's not going to give her this part. He's going to give you this part, because it's your part.

(Jennifer looks at her.)

JENNIFER: *(Hopefully.)* He can't stand her?

MEG: Jennifer, listen to me. Light . . . is emotion.

(Jennifer, calmer, responds to the intensity of Meg's voice. Listens . . .)

MEG: Think of light, a beam of light . . . as a story, a story with its own past, its own history. The light has been who knows where, has illuminated who knows what. Maybe it's been travelling for a long, long time — decades, centuries.

(The lights on them start to dim . . .)

MEG: And somewhere along its journey, it starts to slow down . . . Take a pause, fold into itself . . .

(The lights continue dimming . . .)

MEG: OK, so . . . Now, I want you to imagine you're at the theater. You're sitting in the audience, and you're watching a play. You say you love theater?

JENNIFER: *(Blowing her nose.)* I do. Why are you doing this?

MEG: So the curtain has just opened, and there are three people on stage, and they're still, not moving.

(Lights keep dimming.)

MEG: Who are these people, these characters? What is their past? Their history? We don't know. At the beginning of the play, we don't know anything about them at all. Their pasts are frozen. Suspended.

(The lights stop dimming, and Meg and Jennifer are still for a little while in close to dark.)

MEG: Then the play begins . . . *(Lights start to slowly fade up.)* and we start to learn things about them. Information unfolds. One character leaves. Facts are revealed. We learn that this character really needs something, or this character has a dream, a passion, or maybe this one's been hurt . . . *(A spotlight lights her dimly and gets brighter during the following.)* been hurt really, really badly and we don't know how. Within minutes, we can learn so much about them. In less than ten minutes, we can see the DNA of their whole lives. Even though there are mysteries, we feel we know them, quite well. Then, there comes that moment, that inevitable pivotal moment in a scene when things turn.

MEG: The epiphany. The revelation. Something is illuminated.

(The spotlight on her is very bright now. Other lights are up to half.)

JENNIFER: I think . . . you're probably saying something but I'm not sure what it is.

(Meg looks at her.)

MEG: I think you should put your hair back. Here, take my barrette. *(Meg takes a barrette out of her hair and hands it to Jennifer who puts her hair back.)* That's good. You look . . . like a scientist.

JENNIFER: *(Sympathetically.)* What did Ethan Shroeder do to you that was so bad?

(Meg takes a moment to answer. Jennifer feels badly for her.)

MEG: Nothing terribly original.

JENNIFER: You're not going to read for this part?

MEG: No.

JENNIFER: One thing . . . I do feel emotional, right now.

(A light on Jennifer starts to come up . . . as all other lights start to fade.)

JENNIFER: For you, mainly.

MEG: Use it. But hold it inside. And, I would suggest you drop the accent.

JENNIFER: Really?

MEG: You don't need it. Another thing . . . When you go in there, tell Ethan he looks like a young Richard Burton.

JENNIFER: OK. I can do that. I can do that.

MEG: This is your part.

JENNIFER: *(Confidently, seriously.)* I know. This is my part. This is my part.

(The light on Jennifer grows stronger. All others are out.)

END OF PLAY

The Glory of God

CARSON KREITZER

The Glory of God was commissioned by and
premiered at the Guthrie Theater,
Joe Dowing, Artistic Director.

CHARACTERS

D., Ovid's Daphne: a nymph turning into a tree.

MONK, earnest but with a strong sense of self.

GOATHERD GIRL, fearless, you'd think.

SCHOLAR, intellectual girl, harried. She's lost her data.

TECHIE, kinda cute, very techie.

GIRLFRIEND (DAPHNE), fun and funky, lipstick lesbian. Doubles as the waitress and D.

PRODUCTION NOTE

The Glory of God owes a debt of inspiration to Thomas Cahill's *How the Irish Saved Civilization.*

THE GLORY OF GOD

Lights bang up: we start in a panic. The scholar and the techie.

SCHOLAR: It's gone. Everything's gone. All my —

TECHIE: What am I looking for?

SCHOLAR: *(Slightly crazed.)* The Glory of God.

The icon says The Glory of God.

(Light on D., a nymph. Turning into a tree.)

D.: He is coming. Breath at my back. Catching at my hair. No matter how fast I run, not fast enough. Moments till I am crushed in his large hands. Anything is better than this.

To feel damp mud between my toes and gentle breezes that smell sweet. My hair is leaves my skin is bark I am safe

in here

I am safe

(Light shift: A monk standing at a rudimentary desk, copying from a small book into a large one. Elsewhere, the scholar and the techie, over her laptop.)

SCHOLAR: If not for these wild, barely civilized mountain-dwelling people, all these great texts would have been lost — Plato, Sophocles, everything we know of the ancient world. Copied painstakingly by hand. My monk is a bit of a scamp, actually, adding his own commentary to the margins about various things — the improbability of certain passages in Ovid, sometimes just that he's cold and his hand cramps. He misses the hills above his village. Ireland is still so green and lush, I can't imagine it then. My god, it must have been beautiful.

A lifetime spent copying out texts. Crouched over animal-skin pages, quill and ink —

TECHIE: *(Breaking into her reverie.)* And you didn't back up your hard drive?

SCHOLAR: that's not helpful.

TECHIE: You know what you need? Lunch.

(She looks at him.)

Your computer crashes. Your adrenal glands have been working overtime for a good — six hours?

SCHOLAR: nine.

TECHIE: Nine hours. Your stomach lining is digesting itself at this point. Let me buy you lunch.

SCHOLAR: And then you'll retrieve my data?

TECHIE: to the best of my abilities.

(She begins to hyperventilate.)

see, that doesn't help.

SCHOLAR: neither does your ATTITUDE

TECHIE: and that *really* doesn't help

SCHOLAR: *(Chastened.)* maybe . . . a little something to eat . . . wouldn't be a bad idea.

(Lights shift: the Monk. A girl is just sneaking into the room, through a window. Both have thick, strange but distinctly Irish accents.)

MONK: How can a girl turn into a tree? This makes no sense whatever.

GIRL: *(Landing with a thump.)* I've seen stranger things.

MONK: You're not t'be here.

GIRL: you gonna throw me out?

(He considers for a moment.)

MONK: I will continue with my work and ignore you.

(He does. She is annoyed, then amused.)

GIRL: What're you doing?

MONK: I am looking for the Glory of God.

GIRL: Copying out of a book.

MONK: yes.

GIRL: You think you'll find the Glory of God in there?

MONK: Well that's where I'm looking, or are you deaf as well as rude?

GIRL: Is it a Bible, then, that you're copying?

MONK: It's the tale of a girl who turns into a tree.

GIRL: God turns her into a tree? What's she done, then?

MONK: No, she turns herself into a tree. I think.

To get away from Apollo.

He's Greek.

GIRL: You sure it doesn't say behind a tree?

MONK: No. Turns into a tree. Bark grows over her and everything.

GIRL: Aye, that's what it feels like.

(Monk looks at her.)

I've made myself invisible. To get away from men.

MONK: Does it work?

GIRL: Sometimes.

Sometimes they see you anyway.

(Light shift: the Scholar and the Techie at a table.)

SCHOLAR: The handwriting changes at a certain point. Another monk takes over. A more . . . disciplined copyist. Just the texts, nothing in the margins. These monasteries were subject to periodic attacks. I'm afraid . . . It matches up with the burning of an Abbey at Lindisfarne. And I'm afraid this funny, irreverent young man that I have . . . come to love. I'm afraid he's been killed.

TECHIE: Centuries ago.

SCHOLAR: yes.

TECHIE: And this —

SCHOLAR: Never mind.

TECHIE: bothers you?

SCHOLAR: skip it.

(Beat.)

TECHIE: That's cool.

SCHOLAR: I don't need you to patronize me.

TECHIE: No, it's . . . it's your passion. It's interesting.

It's the same with me. People think it's boring, for most people it *is* boring. But for me, it's like . . . It's like I'm Quincy or something, you know?

SCHOLAR: Yeah!

TECHIE: Like I can find out what happened, I can fix it, I can find it.

SCHOLAR: God, I hope so.

TECHIE: You gotta worry less. This is our relax-you-lunch. Worry less —

SCHOLAR: And back up my hard drive, I know.

(The waitress arrives with lunch. She has an artsy arrangement of twigs in her hair.)

TECHIE: So how come you think he died this horrible way? The book didn't burn, right?

SCHOLAR: It's unmistakable, his writing ends with his last little doggerel poem in the margin. I imagine he scrawled it down before running out to join the fighting. The last lines in his handwriting are:

For I have found the Glory of God and so must write no more.

The Glory of God is in at the window and I am out the door.

TECHIE: The Glory of God is invading Huns?

SCHOLAR: Vikings. And no, it's, you know. Battle. The sanctity of holy battle.

TECHIE: No way he'd be sitting there writing if they're swarming in the window.

SCHOLAR: *(Smiles.)* It's the, uh, noise of the battle. That would be in at the window.

TECHIE: "so must write no more" . . . that's not.

No, if he's going to battle he wouldn't know he won't write anymore. He could survive, come back fine, sit back down at that desk like nothing happened. No, your little Monk is a runaway.

SCHOLAR: Death in battle is certainly a logical assumption —

TECHIE: No, you know what it is?

I've got your Glory of God.

The Glory of God is sunlight.

SCHOLAR: What are you —

TECHIE: In at the window! He sits there at that desk, day in day out. Surrounded by Monks, eating gruel, trapped inside hunched over his work. Hour upon hour. Day upon day. Searching for the Glory of God. And then one day, it hits him. A shaft of light. It's warm on his back, it makes the dust motes shine and dance before his eyes, and suddenly he realizes he doesn't want to be in this subterranean hovel anymore. He doesn't want to be trapped at a desk, nailed down, unable to move, slaving away for this mythical Glory of God when really, it's right outside these walls, grass and clean air and the sun on his face. And he says FUCK IT. I'M OUTTA HERE.

(Beat.)

SCHOLAR: The monastery wouldn't have been subterranean.

TECHIE: A manner of speaking . . .

SCHOLAR: Handy Computer Rescue is subterranean.

(Beat.)

TECHIE: Yeah. I did say subterranean, didn't I.

(Light shift: the Monk and the Girl.)

MONK: I've seen you before.

GIRL: Mmm. I bring the goats milk to the Abbey. An' once I gave it to you. Thought you noticed me then.

(The monk blushes.)

No need to be turnin' red. Y' caught me eye as well. N' I been peekin' in windows ever since, tryin' to find where they'd got you hid.

MONK: What's your name?

GIRL: Used to be Derdriu. Now it's just Girl! See to them goats.

MONK: Derdriu.

GIRL: I like it when you say it.

(Light shift: lunch.)

TECHIE: So, would you wanna do something this weekend?

Provided I retrieve your data and you're still speaking to me?

SCHOLAR: I'm a lesbian.

TECHIE: Whoa! That's not what I was asking.

SCHOLAR: Yes it is.

TECHIE: *(Smiles. Nods.)* OK. It is.

> *(Light shift: the Monk and the Girl. Time has passed. He looks around nervously to make sure they won't be spotted. She walks around his desk with confidence, uncaring.)*

MONK: You don't understand. Nothing made sense till I came here. This is important. What we're doing.

GIRL: Then stay.

MONK: *(Pleading.)* You.

GIRL: I'm going where I never see another goat. We can fish! Live off the bounty of the sea. All God's green land will be ours.

MONK: I can't.

GIRL: And if I'd let a silly thing like that stop me, I'd never a shimmied in that window now, would I?

MONK: It's different for you. You're fearless.

GIRL: *(Soft.)* no. I'm not. *(Strong.)* But nobody's keeping me here another day. I want you to come with me. But I'll go my way without just the same.

> *(Light shift: the Scholar at home with her girlfriend, Daphne.)*

DAPHNE: You let him take you to lunch?
Did you tell him you've got a girlfriend?

SCHOLAR: Yes, actually, I did.

DAPHNE: 'Cuz you figured *that* was more likely to intrigue him, and he'd work harder to get your data back.

SCHOLAR: Daphne!

DAPHNE: You know, for a lesbian feminist, you do make use of those feminine wiles.

SCHOLAR: I don't know what you're talking about.

DAPHNE: How come you don't use 'em on me?

SCHOLAR: *(Relenting.)* You invented 'em. You'd see it coming a mile away.

DAPHNE: AhHa!
An admission of guilt!

SCHOLAR: It's just so hard to negotiate the world. A man would never have to smile, or laugh at anybody's joke, or put in contact lenses.

DAPHNE: You wore contact lenses?

SCHOLAR: No, I barely slept. I was in no condition to think that far ahead.

DAPHNE: But when you got to that counter, the instincts kicked in.

SCHOLAR: Guilty as charged.

DAPHNE: You look cute in your glasses.

SCHOLAR: thanks.

DAPHNE: sexy librarian.

SCHOLAR: Can we have a rational conversation about this?

DAPHNE: Probably not.

SCHOLAR: Actually, I didn't tell him about you.

DAPHNE: You wench!

SCHOLAR: I told him I was a lesbian, but I wanted to leave you out of it, for some reason.

DAPHNE: It's much less fun if you leave me out of it.

SCHOLAR: I didn't want to sully you with his lust.

DAPHNE: Why not?

SCHOLAR: (Looks up smiling.) I'd rather sully you with mine.

DAPHNE: That's more like it. You've been mooning over that goddamn Monk for months. I thought I was gonna have to shave the middle of my head to get your attention.

(Light shift: the Monk and the Girl.)

MONK: Stay here. It's safe.

GIRL: Lindisfarne Abbey was burnt to cinders not a fortnight ago. How's that for God watching over you. I suppose he watches, but doesn't do anything. Has him a little chuckle, you think?

MONK: I must find the Glory of God. My whole life has been —

GIRL: You want the Glory of God?

Come here and I'll show you.

(Places his hand on her breast. He stares at it for a moment, amazed. She pulls his face down to hers. They kiss.)

I'm not leavin' you here.

MONK: No.

GIRL: well lets go then.

MONK: Hang on a minute.

(He goes to the book. Writes something. Light shift brings in the scholar and Daphne.)

SCHOLAR: I just . . . I've got to find what it means.

The Glory of God

DAPHNE: You want the Glory of God?

I'll show you what it means.

(Daphne kisses her.)

SCHOLAR: Be serious.

DAPHNE: Shhhhh. You think I'm not?
   (*Kisses her again. Lights fade on them, leaving the Monk and the Girl. He puts down his quill. Smiles.*)
MONK: all right.

      let's go.
   (*She leads him by the hand, offstage. They pass D., a tree.*)
D.: I hide

      in this bark
      wood pulp
      pages
      scratchings on me. Metal nib and flowing ink
      soft
      like a tiny fingernail on my skin
      I hold these
      secrets

      for a later time
      open me
      crack the binding

      stare
      at these words
      beautiful
      on my
      skin

      shhhhhhhh
      listen.

                    END OF PLAY

The Grand Design

SUSAN MILLER

CHARACTERS

JOSH, mid to late 30s. Smart. Underlying (and not so underlying) angst. Governed by his questions — the joy and difficulty of what he searches for and what he finds — and an abiding sense of humor.

FRANCES, Josh's mother. Late 50s to early 60s. Whatever her son has — trace it back! She is also, like him, in the process of discovery. Their rhythms are bantering, intimate, passionate.

2–3 PEOPLE, any gender. Diverse. They sit somewhere on the periphery of the stage almost as if watching the action until they become part of it.

TIME

The present.

PRODUCTION NOTE

There are three slides shown at the beginning of the play, and one slide near the end.

With a minor adjustment of words in the opening, the play can be done *without* the use of slides.

THE GRAND DESIGN

Lights up. Josh paces, then leans against a desk for ballast. He relishes talking about what he knows and what he struggles to know. A slide goes up. This isn't a lecture. It's an inquiry. An expedition. He is working something out as he talks. In front of us. With us.

JOSH: The first page of the Dutil-Dumas message, sent from a transmitter in the Ukraine. To signal other civilizations. The message was encoded using a system called Lincos that starts with simple mathematical ideas and builds to complex information about who we are. *(Beat.)* In case there's anyone out there. *(Another slide.)* April 5th, 1973. Pioneer 11 is launched into deep space, carrying a message in the form of a six-by-nine-inch gold plaque showing human figures, Earth's location in the universe, and a diagram of the hydrogen atom. *(Beat.)* In that same year, on the day before Pioneer 11 makes its voyage, the ribbon is cut on the tallest building in the world. 110 stories high on sixteen acres in lower Manhattan. "A living representation," according to the architect, "of man's belief in the cooperation of men . . . and through this cooperation his ability to find greatness." *(Another slide.)* November 16th, 1974. The Arecibo Observatory in Puerto Rico sent this message toward a cluster of stars 25,000 light years away. A string of 1,679 bits, or ones and zeros, it can be assembled into a pictogram showing the figure of a man, a telescope, the numbers, DNA, and the solar system. *(End slides.)* 1977. My personal favorite: gold-plated LPs — remember phonograph records? LPs in aluminum cases. Launched on board Voyager I and II. With, of course, instructions on how to play the records. *(He breaks into a dance to a lush arrangement of Sinatra. After a few bars, the music stops. Then, suddenly:)* Items missing from Voyager, Dutil-Dumas, Arecibo, and all previous messages that have traveled through space and time: The Sign over Auschwitz. *Arbeit Macht Frei.* Work makes one free. A slave ship carrying the first of 50 million people Africa will lose to slavery or death, en route. The hole in our ozone layer. A small woman refusing to sit at the back of the bus. Yen. Francs. Dollars. Money.

(A blank slide goes up.)

JOSH: 2003. What? What the fuck's the message this time?

(A woman, Frances, his mother, speaks to the audience from another part of the stage.)

FRANCES: My son is kind of a poet scientist. He's got this grant to come up with a message for alien civilizations. To let them know who we are. The human race. He's hit a wall. And I've left town. On foot.

JOSH: My mother is walking. She's walking with no clear purpose all across the United States. It's her response to the — situation. To turning a certain age. To my breakup. It's her memorial to the nature of our times. *(Beat.)* She calls me from the road.

FRANCES: I'm on the Eleanor Roosevelt Trail. *(A succession of calls.)* I'm standing outside a church on top of a hill in Ohio where the Underground Railroad connected. *(Beat.)* I don't know where I am. But, I see cows. I'm covering ground. I'm walking past the things I know. I met this person who picks the places to stop along the way. You know when you get directions — on your computer. What's that called — map something? Well, they actually send people out to find interesting things to do along the routes. I just never thought of that. There are all kinds of jobs I never thought about.

JOSH: Look, I'm sorry. I'm sorry things didn't work out and I didn't give you grandchildren and —

FRANCES: *(To audience.)* He thinks I'm out here because he failed in his marriage. I'm out here because I failed. To know what to do next. I was sad. And I started walking. I was walking in circles all around the house. Finally, I just took it outside. And I'm not the only one out here. There are mothers walking all over the place. *(Beat.)* I'm worried he won't find love. *(The phone rings in his house. Although they begin talking to each other, as if on the phone, this is dropped shortly and they just address each other directly.)*

FRANCES: Hi, Sweetie!

JOSH: Mom? Where are you?

FRANCES: If I wanted to be located, I would stay home.

JOSH: Are you just walking aimlessly or do you have some kind of plan?

FRANCES: I do have a plan. To walk aimlessly. All right, the story so far. I just had pie. They use shortening and whole eggs and I don't care. Because while I eat my pie and have my coffee, I'm not drowning in the facts. There is no true history of the United States. I am not guilty. I am not wanting. I am not disappointed. So, how are you coming with your memo to alien civilizations?

JOSH: See, when you say it like that —

FRANCES: Like what?

JOSH: Like how you said it.

FRANCES: Like how I said memo or how's it coming?

JOSH: How you said it like you had no opinion or no opinion you'd be ready to reveal, even though we can be pretty sure that you are always in possession of an opinion. Anyhow, I'm not writing a memo. It's more like an equation. You know? Which lays out the thing to be discovered or proven. It's not necessarily what we are — it's what we could be.

FRANCES: *(Struck.)* That's lovely.

JOSH: For a lie, you mean.

FRANCES: Maybe it's a lie we need.

JOSH: Well, I do, I guess. I need it. *(Beat.)* See, the big discoveries — gravity, particle theory, chaos, DNA — they place us. They put us in the physical world. But they're just descriptions. Of our physical properties. Our propensities. What we're capable of — what's possible, what we've already accomplished, I mean how do you — First . . . I thought, well, fucking, of course. Sexual congress. For them to see how we do it and how much we like to do it. But, fucking causes so much confusion and anxiety. And what if they interpret two figures expressing their ardor as some kind of cruel rite? And the truth is, fucking doesn't last. And, then, what about madness, disorders of the mind, bodies that aren't whole? *(Beat.)* I should just tell them to be human is to impose yourself on the world. This is how I see it, so this is how it is.

FRANCES: *(A beat.)* Or — you could take this grant money and give it away to actual people. So they could eat, go to school, and maybe collectively expand and redefine the concept of what it is to be human.

JOSH: OK, sister, listen, didn't I give up my beautiful SUV when you were on your moral imperative not to drive big gas guzzling automobiles thus entrenching us in a relationship with oil-producing nations and consequently undermining what we tout to be our own unique position of being free in the world?

FRANCES: I was quoting. I didn't come up with that myself, which is disturbing, because I don't always see how things fit, and I'm always completely thrown to learn there's this relationship between a simple thing like buying a car or a carton of milk and the decline of civilization.

JOSH: Well, just put your two cents in about this, would you, and help me out here. I mean, is it sentimental to think there's something — anything — we have in common with everyone else on earth?

FRANCES: What everyone wants to know is who am I going to be? And then, who am I going to be with who'll make it not so terrible to *be* me. And if you have children, well, who are they going to be and who are they going to be with and will I like who they are and who they're with and how do I keep them safe? *(Beat.)* Maybe you're reaching, Josh. Maybe the story of one person is all they need to know about us.

JOSH: Where the hell are you?

FRANCES: In my tent.

JOSH: You are not in any kind of a tent.

FRANCES: In my tent outside of my room at the motel. You don't think I'd really pee in the open, do you? You should go outside. It is an alarmingly beautiful night.

JOSH: I can't go outside. I can't think outside.

FRANCES: Did you open my letter yet?

JOSH: *(Avoiding.)* I haven't had a chance — actually.

FRANCES: I know you're carrying it around in your pocket and it's getting smushed and I need you to read it.

JOSH: I know you want me to read it, Frances. So it must be important. And that, of course, brings up my morbid fear of important letters.

FRANCES: Josh.

JOSH: And I don't really have the time right now.

FRANCES: *(Retreating.)* OK.

JOSH: I'm in over my head with this thing.

FRANCES: Look, if the aliens have a sense of humor, they'll see the irony. Or they'll receive it like the French do when you try to speak in their language. *(A beat.)* Tell me . . . just show me what you've got so far.

JOSH: Just — you know, I'm still working on it.

(After a moment, an actor steps forward from another part of the stage and stands with arms outstretched — or Josh manipulates him into this position, framed by the light of the slide projections, to represent a living slide show of Josh's work in progress.)

JOSH: That we're — incomplete. That we long for. That we miss our chances. And we're born to repeat: If only. If only!

(A second actor comes forward and joins hands with the first.)

FRANCES: How it is to hold someone else's life in your own. *(Beat.)* Can you add a dog? I think we need them, somehow.

(The actor holds the other in his arms, as if he were wounded or ailing, in need.)

JOSH: That we're moved. That we can meet another person's sorrow or subjugation with an answering cry and a wish to make it better. Not because we're thinking, "that could be me" but because that is me. *(Beat.)* You know, if you put a group of six-month-old babies in a room and one starts to cry, pretty soon they all start crying. They can't differentiate. They are all one living, breathing, wailing, sobbing, suffering being.

(Another actor joins them. They stand still. Only their expressions change, illustrating different reactions to something we don't see.)

JOSH: The chemistry of the brain changes with certain events. Once you witness an atrocity — or hear a cruel remark. When you cause the disappointment in someone's eyes. Or see an act of courage. There's a shift. Now your brain's accommodating this new information. You're still pulled to the earth by gravity. And your blood type is still O positive. But what happens to other people is placing itself in your cells. It resides in you now. And you're not the same. It changes you forever.

(The actors move to the rear of the stage, where they sit.)

FRANCES: Come outside. Be with me, tonight.

(After a moment, he walks "outside." They both stand under a starry sky. Josh looks up toward the heavens, addressing the unknown civilizations.)

JOSH: OK, I have some questions for *you*! Do you have pets? Do you marry? Is there gender? Does it matter to you if another of your species, group, tribe, community, has different markings? Do you have prisons? Are you kind? Do you sleep? Do you have mothers?

FRANCES: *(Joins him in shouting out to the universe.)* This is who we are! Hurtling through time, tumbling, stretching, moving through time to what we're meant to be. This is us. Becoming! *(Beat — to Josh.)* Please open the envelope.

JOSH: *(A moment.)* Fine.

(He retrieves the letter from his pocket and opens it.)

JOSH: I see something that looks like a house. And little stick figures in crayon.

FRANCES: The other side.

(He turns it over and starts to read out loud.)

JOSH: The last will and testament of — *(As he realizes what it is.)* — my one and only mother! Jesus. I don't want to see this. I don't want to think about it.

FRANCES: Well, you have to.

JOSH: Why? Why do I have to? I don't have to.

FRANCES: You're my executor, beneficiary, and medical proxy. And when you have children —

JOSH: Would you please — with the children.

FRANCES: It could happen.

JOSH: Are you all right? Should I be worried? I'm worried.

FRANCES: I'm fine. It's just something a person has to do. I'm all right.

(A beat. As Josh looks over the will. And turns it over.)

JOSH: So, what's this drawing?

FRANCES: Something you did when you were around five, I think. You drew a house. Next to other houses. Because you said our house needs those other houses. So you drew a house with people inside. Small people. And big people to take care of them, to give them an example, to accompany them on their way. *(Beat.)* My god, you were so — *(As it comes to her.)* Smart. Josh. What makes us human is other humans.

(A moment.)

JOSH: *(To audience.)* After my mother dies, some years from now, and I've married my first wife all over again. And a simple child's drawing has gone into space — I tell my daughter the story of one person. Walking. Looking at things. Listening to other people's stories. Wanting to know.

(He turns back to Frances. They are on their phones again.)

FRANCES: *(So full, it can be understated.)* I love you, Josh. I love you so much.

(The slide of Josh's childhood drawing goes up.)

OTHER ACTORS: *(Each speaks a line in turn.)* In Wonder. In Awe. In Loss. In Gratitude. In Sympathy. In Release. In Pain. In Memory. In Celebration. In Mourning. In Difficulty. In our Stumble and Fall. In each Attempt. In Remission. In Rapture. In the Beginning. In the End. In IT.

JOSH: *(Beat.)* I love you, too, mom.

(The light narrows to frame the drawing. Until, lights fade.)

END OF PLAY

The Joy of
Having a Body

JULIE MARIE MYATT

The Joy of Having a Body was commissioned and
premiered at the Guthrie Theater,
Joe Dowling, Artistic Director.

CHARACTERS

ANNA

STEVE

MANNY

TED

JIM

SETTING

Light. A bare stage except for a wooden chair. A large pair of white wings sits on top of the chair.

TIME

Now.

THE JOY OF HAVING A BODY

EVENING WITHOUT ANGELS
the great interest of man: air and light,
the joy of having a body,
the voluptuousness of looking.

Mario Rossi

Ted and Jim lay on the floor, on top of each other. Then Anna, then Steve and
Manny lay on top of her. (Anna is in-between them like a sandwich. She
wears a bra and panties.) The stage is bare except for a large pair of wings
that sits on a simple wooden chair in the corner.

ANNA: OK. That's good. Very good. Nice. Good going boys.
(The men begin to stand up, to free her.)
ANNA: Wow. Great stuff. I like that. Very nice. We should do that more often.
STEVE: Why?
ANNA: Why not?
JIM: Well, what's it for?
ANNA: I want you to all line up in a row.
TED: Why?
ANNA: Jiminy Christmas. 'Why' this? 'Why' that? Line up.
(The men line up. Facing her. Anna walks around them.)
ANNA: Uh-huh . . . uh-huh . . . Good. Now. Let me see your stomachs.
MEN: Again?
ANNA: Lift up your shirts.
STEVE: Why —?
ANNA: Lift!
(The men reluctantly lift their shirts.)
ANNA: Hmm . . . well . . . yes . . . there you are. I suppose that will have to do,
won't it. Ted, suck it in.
TED: I am.
(Anna touches his stomach. Kisses his lips.)
ANNA: Hmm . . . well then . . . perhaps . . . just, just keep the lights out.
(She proceeds to touch each one of the men's stomachs.)

ANNA: Oh yes. Nice, Steve . . . very nice . . . firm . . . I see some men actually take my advice.

STEVE: Like you say, it's wild, it's tough out there —

ANNA: Those sit-ups are indeed paying off. Bring on the wash! *(She scrubs his belly. Steve blushes. She moves on to Manny.)* Oh my. Manny, my my my . . . your skin is certainly very soft.

MANNY: That oil you gave me really works —

(She places her own stomach against his.)

ANNA: Yes. Oh yes. Indeed. She'll like this.

MANNY: I think so — I really hope so —

ANNA: Very much. *(Anna reluctantly pulls away.)*

TED: Anna, I'm sorry, but . . . but, uh . . . how much longer do we have to go through this?

ANNA: Until you get it right.

TED: Get what right? We've done Everything Known to Man —

STEVE: Enthusiastically tackling menial domestic chores.

TED: Marriage counselling. When to buy diamonds —

MANNY: Chakra release, cross-country skiing, Tantric sex practices —

JIM: And it's getting boring.

(The other men look at Jim. Nervous.)

ANNA: What? I'm sorry, but I thought you said — what did you say?

JIM: I said, it's get — getting —

ANNA: "BORING." . . . I have every right mind to keep you here.

(The other men jump to attention.)

ANNA: So . . . You want to stay? Is that what you want? Huh?

JIM: No —

ANNA: I can arrange that. I can get you back that leash to eternity in two seconds flat —

JIM: No, no. I swear. I, I didn't mean to say — I just —

ANNA: There is Never a moment when this "is getting boring." Never. You hear me?

MEN: Yes.

ANNA: JIM?

JIM: Loud, loud and clear. Anna.

ANNA: Anna who —

JIM: Anna my love —

ANNA: THIS is what you're going down there for. Am I correct?

MEN: Yes.

ANNA: THIS is what you're being sent to do. Correct?

TED: What, what about talking?

ANNA: Talking?

TED: Aren't we going to talk?

ANNA: Of course you are.

TED: I'd kind of like to have a nice conversation with her.

ANNA: Well, yes, Ted. Where have you been? That's expected —

TED: Then, then why have we spent all this time rubbing up against you, and flexing our muscles, and kissing your back?

ANNA: Oh . . . well . . . that was nice, wasn't it? Maybe we should do that again, just for —

STEVE: We were supposed to leave four days ago.

MANNY: Five. Actually.

JIM: More like twelve —

ANNA: Since when do we work in, in DAYS?

STEVE: Well —

ANNA: Time means nothing to us —

STEVE: But you said we were being rushed —

ANNA: Listen, this, this mission — this opportunity is not to be taken lightly. We have a serious problem down there.

JIM: We have all the moves, all the data now, lamaze and —

ANNA: We've got ourselves a situation.

TED: Let us go take care of —

STEVE, JIM, MANNY: Yeah —

ANNA: It's of a magnitude that only We — well I — could intercept. Sure, they could've called the archs, the principalities, the dominions, the thrones — pffsh — though everyone knows they wouldn't really give a rat's ass, sitting up there on their high horse —

JIM: I'm a throne —

ANNA: They could've called the cherubs. Why not. They get all the good press. All those bare-assed paintings and rosey-cheeked smiles. Harps galore. Those jokers can't even hold a note, you know —

TED: I'm a cherub —

ANNA: They went straight to the top — who, who did they call? Hmm?
(The men are silent.)

ANNA: *(Whispers.)* Seraphim.
(All the men roll their eyes, behind her back.)

ANNA: We put the high in celestial hierarchy. I'm cream of the crop, boys. God's girl. Top of the heap. I've reached the spiritual cathedral ceiling. I'm infinite. And they called me. Why?

STEVE: You were available?

(The men laugh.)

ANNA: That's beside the point —

JIM: And you do have some terrific legs —

MANNY: Really. Everybody says so —

ANNA: Because there is a serious situation at hand down there and they called in the TOP GUNS to handle it.

(The men are still giggling.)

ANNA: Take off your pants.

(The men stop laughing.)

TED: Again?

JIM: Why?

ANNA: Hey! We've got a situation! Don't argue with me!

(The men take off their pants.)

ANNA: When you have got women turned inside out down there . . . when they're dying their hair and crying on each other's shoulders . . . when every conversation turns to yet another male disappointment and lackluster event under the sheets . . . when they would rather get drunk alone on an expensive bottle of wine than go get smashed at a bar and go home with a "decent enough" looking stranger . . . when they begin freezing their eggs because they can't meet one man who will commit to sit on the damn nest with them . . . you've not just got yourself a situation, you've got yourself a crisis.

MANNY: But —

ANNA: A CRISIS!

STEVE: We know what we're up against —

ANNA: You have been chosen boys.

MANNY: I replaced someone, actually —

ANNA: CHOSEN! Among millions! Light years of men. For a most courageous job. America's future depends on you. A battle —

JIM: Let me go win it —

STEVE, TED, MANNY: Yeah, let us go —

ANNA: Against lost hope. You have got to go down there and be TRIUMPHANT. You have got to RESTORE FAITH! Yes. Faith! You have got to go down there and go where no man has gone . . . "in a very long time." You have to be limitless, boys; emotionally available and sexually ambitious, all wrapped in one warm delicious commitment . . . You have to be Home Sweet Home — Take off your shirts.

MANNY: But —

ANNA: You, you think the Devil's our Nemesis? Our red-headed stranger, perched on the other side of every shoulder? Be ready to meet FEAR! I'm telling you, you have got to go down there and outweigh FEAR. FEAR?! You know how hard that is?

(The men begin to answer —)

ANNA: It's like trying to spin that earth in the opposite direction. Like stopping a train with your tooth. Like refolding a map in one go. Are you ready for that, boys? Really ready? . . . Steve?

STEVE: "You can trust me . . . Please trust me?"

(Anna walks closer to him, nodding. She gently touches his neck, his shoulders.)

ANNA: You have got to be all that they have lost faith in.

STEVE: "I'm not going to leave you for someone younger."

(She moves over to Manny. Touches his stomach.)

ANNA: All that they are afraid of doesn't exist anymore.

MANNY: "I am listening to you. I'm listening to what you don't say."

ANNA: All that their bodies crave.

MANNY: "Where shall I touch you first?"

(She moves on to Jim.)

ANNA: All that they've missed so very much.

JIM: "You're the one I want to marry. How many kids shall we have? Oh, let's have a big family."

(She looks the men over as she moves to Ted.)

ANNA: Great men.

TED: "Hand me your heart."

MEN: "I'm here. Bold. I won't desert you."

ANNA: You must be . . . Earth's most glorious gift . . . solace . . .

MEN: "I'm not afraid of you."

(She lays her head on Ted's chest. Ted touches her hair. Lovingly.)

ANNA: Heaven's pleasures on human flesh. Oh dear sweet skin. (I miss you.) The happy calm. The body's song. Lullabies they don't want to forget . . .

MEN: "Come closer. Come closer. Open up . . . Lean into me."

ANNA: The swaying backs . . . limbs together . . . breath held . . . chorus.

MEN: "Don't be afraid. I love you. You're not alone. (*The men all reach for her.*) You're not alone."

(Anna slowly lifts her head off Ted's chest. Then quickly. Gathers herself.)

ANNA: Oh. Yes. Well. Yes. I think you're ready for the job. Yes. Jeez. Of course you're ready. Yes. Sure. Time is wasting.

(The men begin to gather their clothes.)

JIM: It's a crisis, right? We really better get out there.

MANNY: They're waiting, right?

STEVE: You've . . . you've trained us well. We're your men.

TED: Absolutely.

MANNY: You're the best.

MEN: Absolutely.

ANNA: Sure. Yes . . . It's been fun, huh?

JIM: Anything but boring . . . I'll make you proud, Anna. I guarantee it. New York is in excellent hands. I will still the chaos . . . the ground will be New . . . Thanks to you —

(He touches her face. She turns away.)

ANNA: Go on. Make them weep with joy now.

(Jim exits.)

ANNA: Washington?

(Steve salutes. Tries to speak. Reaches to kiss her instead.)

ANNA: Let there be nothing conservative about you. LIBERATE THEM. *(She brushes him away. He kisses her back, then exits.)* Los Angeles? Hurray for Hollywood?

TED: I'm your star. Tom Cruise has got nothing on —

ANNA: "You had me at hello."

(Ted smiles and exits.)

ANNA: And my dear Manny — you're my favorite you know — but don't tell the rest — *(Anna puts her arm around him.)* Are you sure you're ready for Minneapolis? I hear they Really need you out there —

(He pulls a scarf from his shorts. Quickly wraps it around his neck —)

ANNA: Run.

(Manny runs off the stage. Anna sees her wings, waiting for her on the chair. She slowly walks over to them. They are heavy; she struggles to put them back on her back, but succeeds. She is a magnificent sight in her wings! She stands looking at a pair of socks left behind, then takes a seat on the chair. She feels an itch, and scratches her wing.)

END OF PLAY

The New New

KELLY STUART

The New New was commissioned by and
premiered at the Guthrie Theater,
Joe Dowling, Artistic Director.

THE NEW NEW

Jenny and Marcy in one "office" area — they are stapling brochures or doing some other type of repetitive office work. Bradley and Craig in another office — they are actually separated by a long corridor, but should be represented as being in isolated areas of the stage.

JENNY: I'm going to have an affair with him.

MARCY: But Jenny, you're failing his class.

JENNY: He says I can take an incomplete if I want, and he'll help me make it up over the summer.

BRADLEY: I need a new word for new.

CRAIG: Fresh.

BRADLEY: Too hip hop. This is more white.

CRAIG: *(Opening a thesaurus.)* Thesaurus check.

(Naomi, a nervous, down-at-the-heels woman appears and stands, hoping to engage Marcy and Jenny's attention.)

MARCY: Isn't he what, like, uh, married?

JENNY: Yeah, but we have this INTENSE CONNECTION. It's like, ECO-NOMICS is not my forte. I find the whole subject abysmal. But he's got this precision of mind and I want that. I think that's what's missing in me, and I'm so, like, attracted to that.

NAOMI: I'm here to see Bradley Zuckerman?

(Jenny and Marcy look at her, deciding she's a nonentity.)

CRAIG: *(Reading.)* Fresh, modern. Modernistic. Neoteric.

BRADLEY: Neoteric?

(They shrug in unison. Craig continues.)

CRAIG: Novel. Newfangled. Newsprung. Revived. Reinvigorating.

BRADLEY: ". . . Reinvigorated the genre of prison memoir."

CRAIG: That's stale.

BRADLEY: It's become stale to say something is NEW. What's the new new? We need the new NEW.

MARCY: Did you ask me a question?

NAOMI: Bradley Zuckerman?

MARCY: Do you have an appointment?

NAOMI: When is he back?

MARCY: Do you have an appointment?

NAOMI: When is he back?

JENNY: Do you have an appointment?

NAOMI: I'll wait.

MARCY: We discourage that.

JENNY: He's not coming in. He's with marketing. So you would simply be wasting your time.

NAOMI: Where's marketing?

(Marcy turns back to Jenny, leaving Naomi standing awkwardly. They whisper to each other, occasionally looking Naomi's way. Naomi watches. They giggle.)

BRADLEY: A laser-sharp vision. The voice. The, something, vision and voice. His. New. The . . . What. There's no more words.

CRAIG: I liked Neoteric.

BRADLEY: Nobody will know what that means.

CRAIG: A powerful neoteric account, of the agony behind prison walls.

BRADLEY: I'm sorry, that sounds like gobbledygook. Um . . . deadpan, self-deprecating and, witty. But it's also new and it's important we say that.

CRAIG: It's a first novel.

BRADLEY: It's a memoir.

CRAIG: Actually, we can't call it a memoir. It's a kind of memoiristic novel.

BRADLEY: Why can't we call it a memoir?

CRAIG: Legal affairs said —

BRADLEY: OK it's a novel in the form of a memoir, based on real-life authentic experience.

(Naomi continues to stand looking at the women. They ignore her. Their conversation has become audible again:)

JENNY: There is like, so much electricity there. When he's looking at me, it's like I get zapped.

MARCY: Well I really want you to meet this guy.

JENNY: The writer?

MARCY: Yeah. Jimmy.

BRADLEY: The absurdity and the agony of life as a convict.

CRAIG: Agony isn't a word that sells.

BRADLEY: Agonizing, and yet entertaining.

CRAIG: That sounds so *People* magazine.

(They scan a thesaurus.)

JENNY: What does he write about?

MARCY: Um, prison. Jail. The Penal system.

JENNY: Oh.

MARCY: He had like, an MBA from Yale but I think he was like, convicted of manslaughter.

JENNY: Oh. A murderer.

MARCY: Manslaughter. I think. It was accidental. Self Defense. Some kind of fight, with this guy named monster. This six foot two, three hundred pound monster. An accidental death that he was convicted of — I guess, I guess, he pled guilty.

JENNY: Oh.

MARCY: To spare something, more like, the death penalty. I mean, I guess he cut a deal.

(Jenny notices Naomi staring at her.)

JENNY: Can we help you with something else?

NAOMI: Who are you talking about?

MARCY: I'm going to have to ask you to leave, OK?

NAOMI: I need to see Bradley Zuckerman.

MARCY: Leave a number and go or I'll have to call security.

NAOMI: I'd like to know who you're talking about.

JENNY: Did you not hear us? Do we HAVE to call security?

(Naomi abruptly leaves. The two women shake their heads in disgust.)

MARCY: These people will do anything to make you take a manuscript. Anyway he's — he's just really charismatic and charming and smart. I mean, it is so odd, when you meet him, you'll see, what an odd juxtaposition to think of this guy in prison. I mean, I'm really FOND of him. And his writing is really super evocative of the, you know, of the Kafkaesque nature of life in prison. He's sexy too.

JENNY: So why don't you sleep with him?

MARCY: I'm trying to be monogamous now. And Bradley is like, editing his book. I can't do that. Sleep with the guy Bradley edits.

(Naomi makes a cross past the stage. Disappears.)

BRADLEY: I used to get these calls from prison, collect calls every Tuesday. I thought of these calls as my "Tuesdays with Jimmy." He was just this witty, sardonic ethnographer of prison life. Of the ingenuity. And the angle, the engagement I found with the theme of this — civilized business executive locked up with all these illiterate thugs, and how he survived.

CRAIG: I love that he used like, sales techniques.

BRADLEY: Yes.

CRAIG: Stuff he learned from corporate sales seminars: Body language mirroring.

BRADLEY: I guess it all works.

(*For a beat, they mirror each other's body language. Naomi enters and stares at them. They ignore her.*)

CRAIG: In a way it doesn't matter how we market this thing because film rights have already gone to Ben Stiller.

BRADLEY: Really?

CRAIG: Mike Medavoy loved it. The release will coincide with the movie.

BRADLEY: But that's . . . I mean, there's a literary value.

CRAIG: It's great. Ben Stiller.

BRADLEY: Ben Stiller. That's great.

NAOMI: Excuse me —

CRAIG: It's a comedy. That's how they see it. It's going to sell like a motherfucker.

NAOMI: Is this marketing?

CRAIG: Yes.

NAOMI: I'm looking for Bradley Zuckerman.

CRAIG: Bradley —

BRADLEY: He doesn't work here. You have the wrong department.

NAOMI: I was told he's in marketing.

MARCY: I just think you'd have more in common with him than with your economics professor.

JENNY: Why? Because he's a criminal?

MARCY: But he's not really.

BRADLEY: No, uh, he works in creative development.

NAOMI: But they said in his office that he was in here.

BRADLEY: No. He's not here. Have you seen him Craig?

CRAIG: Haven't seen him.

BRADLEY: Would you like to leave a message for him?

CRAIG: I'm sorry. You really can't wait here. Would you like to leave him a message? (*He hands her a notepad. She stands looking at it. She begins to write, furiously.*)

MARCY: Being convicted of manslaughter had nothing to do with the arc of his life. It was just, this aberration.

JENNY: Who did he kill again?

MARCY: This drug dealer guy. You're going to like him. I told him about you, he's interested in meeting you.

JENNY: So he's like, — out?

MARCY: On Parole.

(*Naomi has finished writing.*)

NAOMI: Will you make sure Bradley Zuckerman gets this?

BRADLEY: Certainly.

(Naomi gives them the pad of paper and exits. The men giggle.)

BRADLEY: Oh my God that was close.

CRAIG: "No I'm not Bradley."

BRADLEY: "BRADLEY? NO. I HAVEN'T SEEN HIM." Anyway, Jesus. What does she want? *(Craig is reading the pad of paper. He hands it to Bradley.)* My brother's name was Jeremy. Not Monster. He was five foot three, one hundred thirty pounds. Not six foot two, three hundred fifty. My brother was tortured and strangled over the course of a two-hour, period. The shape of a turtle and a steer were imprinted on my brother's neck, from the cowboy belt your so-called "author" used. My brother's face was badly beaten, bones protruded from his bloody face. My brother was a medical assistant. He was a human being, not a monster. To see this man profit, it's killing me and I wonder if you ever gave that a thought?

CRAIG: I still think, um. The SPIRIT of the — I mean, he was true to the SPIRIT of, the book's not about the crime in any case and uh, legally, there's no . . .

BRADLEY: You knew this?

CRAIG: It's not really an issue.

BRADLEY: I mean, the thing of it is, I — I really like Jimmy.

CRAIG: Yeah, and who is she? Who is she really? Like what do you know?

BRADLEY: And the thing of it is, it's about Jimmy's writing. I think his writing redeems him.

CRAIG: Yeah. That's why we never, like bothered to check.

MARCY: You know it's already been optioned as a movie? For Ben Stiller.

JENNY: I love Ben Stiller.

MARCY: Then I think, really, you're going to love Jimmy.

BRADLEY: I'm fixing him up with my girlfriend's sister. I wouldn't do that if I didn't like him, if I thought he was wasn't, a good person. Yeah. It's fine. It's.

CRAIG: I mean, — this . . . — like, she's the victim's sister. That's all. What do you expect?

JENNY: So, what are we going to do, like, go out to dinner together? Are we —

MARCY: Yeah.

JENNY: I'm up for that.

(Bradley looks seriously confused. Lights fade.)

END OF PLAY

PLAYS FOR SIX
OR MORE ACTORS

The Thief of Man

KEVIN KLING

The Thief of Man was commissioned by and
premiered at the Guthrie Theater,
Joe Dowling, Artistic Director.

CHARACTERS

KNIGHT, a Viking warrior.

MAK, his servant.

TEMPLAR, a knight of the Holy Order.

NUN, a nun of the Christian (Greek) Orthodox.

INNKEEPER, a Turk.

DAUGHTER, his daughter.

DEATH, death.

TIME

1204 A.D.

PLACE

Constantinople, during the fourth Holy Crusade

THE THIEF OF MAN

KNIGHT: Help me Mak. I'm gored.

MAK: I have you, my lord.

KNIGHT: My legs under me fold as lapped in a tempest.

MAK: Help. Sir, something to drink, your best.

INNKEEPER: Right away.

KNIGHT: My wound be fatal fair, Mak.

MAK: No. A nick is all.

KNIGHT: How come we under attack?

MAK: I know not we were fell upon by crusaders.

KNIGHT: Where is The White Bear?

MAK: Gone. Escaped I fear.

KNIGHT: No.

MAK: Sh. Sh. We will find him soon enough.

KNIGHT: Not I. My candle's snuft.

TEMPLAR: Be you Christian? Do you seek last rites?

MAK: Norsemen.

TEMPLAR: A Viking?

MAK: Aye, This best of warrior's soul takes flight
    From this putrid land Hot as hell
    and food so spiced one cannot tell
    flesh from root
    Oh, God
    for a cod
    and a fur-lined boot

TEMPLAR: Why didst they attack him thus?

MAK: We had a White Bear with us from our homeland. To be presented as a gift
    to his lordship of Constantinople. This much my master told the Crusaders
    yet they fell upon him saying "it is now property of the Pope." "Are they not
    both Christians born all of the same Virgin?" quoth my Master.
    "Stand aside," quoth they.

MAK: My Master drew his sword but there were too many. I cut the Bear loose
    to cover our escape. Oh Master forgive me.

KNIGHT: You are good fair Mak.

INNKEEPER: Here you are, sir. May Allah show mercy to your friend. And you, sire Templar.

MAK: Ahhhh, A Templar, sir, a Crusader. Puke. Bile. Wretch. Phlegm. Scum. Slime. Scab. Flatus. Turd. Puss. Piss. . . . Shoat.

TEMPLAR: Shoat?

MAK: Aye, Shoat. Shoat of shoats, Image, extract and essence of shoat, Shoat of shoat hall. Lord, master and sire of all that is shoat.

TEMPLAR: Please good sir. I have no ill will toward you. I am not in league with this new Crusade.

KNIGHT: Ahhh . . . *(He babbles in an ancient Icelandic tongue.)*

TEMPLAR: He swims in dreams now and treads for his life.

MAK: My dear master.

Let you go, Welcome the Valkyries that will gently swoop down for your brave soul and whisk you to Valhalla.

Sweet pipes will beguile your cares, and as is your Viking right, will you now make love with the blessed angel of death.

Let go brave one, tis your birthright to rest now in the buxomness of your ancestors.

DAUGHTER: Papa, someone was outside asking for this place.

MAK: The thief of man.

INNKEEPER: Where? I see no one.

DAUGHTER: I said we lived elsewhere.

INNKEEPER: Good child.

MAK: Only a child can lie to death and get away with it.

TEMPLAR: Or a drunk.

MAK: True.

MAK AND TEMPLAR: Or a drunk.

MAK: Innkeeper another.

TEMPLAR: Innkeeper here too.

MAK: I fear Death has come for my master.

NUN: No, it is for me.

TEMPLAR: You Sister? Are you wounded?

NUN: My wound goes deeper to the immortal soul.

Two months past Crusaders overran my abbey in Zara, another christian city. Although under strict orders from the Pope to leave all life and not pillage the sacred temples, they attacked like mad dogs killing the monks and plundering the sanctuaries. Our Holy Relics now rest in Venetian ships.

MAK: What of you, Sister?

NUN: I, like my Sisters, was also violated.

TEMPLAR: This cannot be. Men of God? What said the Holy Father to this?

NUN: The word from Pope Innocent is that the crusaders are absolved from sin because those killed are labeled infidel and the sooner dispatched from earth, the sooner purified in hell's fire. As for their attack on the Sisters, the Pope has declared the Crusaders absolved from sin for they were spreading holy seed and offer hope to the future.

MAK: This Pope lives for the word not by the word.

NUN: When I felt life grow inside of me I came to Constantinople for a powder that will help restore me to the Holy Order. This powder have I taken and its affects are most severe. I fear two souls may be washed from the earth. I am the one death seeks in order to meet my true husband if he will have me.

TEMPLAR: Sister, I am sorry yet I am the one death seeks. I am returned from the Holy Land where I fought bravely beside Richard in his campaign against Saladin. I wear the red cross of the Templars. Our sect has become strong and powerful. I love my brothers. But the love we share goes beyond the brotherly love defined by the church. This the pope knows and will one day use it to destroy us. One day we will be declared heretic.

MAK: Tis true, to calm the masses People need a little devil inside the gates as well as outside.

TEMPLAR: This is our most sacred object. As long as this is in our possession the Pope dare not touch us. In this bag is the Head of Christ.

MAK: It is a head. And it's old.

TEMPLAR: I am returning to France but the years in the Holy Land have left me frail. I have been scorched raw, starved and bloodied. A leaf that grows too far from the trunk of a tree grows weak. I fear now I die of a sickness and I have no power against it.

INNKEEPER: It is not you Templar, or you Sister, it is me. I have lost a wife and two sons to the recent seige. At times a great pain takes my chest. This is not the first time my daughter has talked death from this gate. It is Allah's will and my joy I join my loved ones.

NUN: No it is me.

TEMPLAR: I'm sure I am the one.

MAK: My Master.

INNKEEPER: Maybe it is all of us.

MAK: Perhaps it is none.

KNIGHT: Maybe 'twas not death at all.

EVERYONE: Aye.

(Death enters.)

DEATH: An audience.

DAUGHTER: The thief of man.

MAK: Master be brave.

INNKEEPER: Have you come for one of us?

DEATH: I have.

NUN: I am ready.

TEMPLAR: As am I.

MAK: Master, be strong.

DEATH: You Mak.

MAK: Me? I am in no pain.

DEATH: That is why it must be you. To feel pain is to be alive.

MAK: I am a little hungry.

DEATH: Mak, You were killed beside your Master; You died bravely and with honor.

MAK: That was an hour ago.

DEATH: Forgive me this has been a busy day. I have not been able to reach you till now.

MAK: Dear Sister, I will speak with your husband. I am to believe he is very understanding and will welcome you with open arms.

SISTER: Thank you kind sir.

MAK: And I will tell him his heart and his head are in good hands.

TEMPLAR: I thank you.

MAK: So long good master.

KNIGHT: Good-bye Mak. I will join you soon.

DEATH: You are a Viking.

MAK: Yes. And you are the Angel of death.

DEATH: That is true.

MAK: To Valhalla?

DEATH: Yes. But good Mak let us take our time.

DAUGHTER: Father I saw a White Bear.

INNKEEPER: Tell me daughter.

DAUGHTER: This large White Bear from a land of cold and ice.
    Ran through the streets.
    The people tried to stab the bear but it would not die.
    The heat made the bear sick but it would not die.

When it ate its fill the bear drank from below the ground where the water runs black.

This satisfied the bear.

INNKEEPER: When will the bear go home?

DAUGHTER: When there is nothing more to drink.

END OF PLAY

Pleasure Cruise

KIRA OBOLENSKY

Pleasure Cruise was commissioned by and
premiered at the Guthrie Theatre,
Joe Dowling, Artistic Director.

CHARACTERS

MAN

WOMAN

Various roles including waiter, person, voice, riverboat captain, Jack, which can be played by a variety of actors, or one actor.

PLACE

A pleasure craft, of a sort.

TIME

The present.

PRODUCTION NOTES

When the word "Pleasure" is mentioned, it becomes a kind of reenactment, however subtle, of the sensory experience of pleasure. I intend for the "pleasure parts" to be verbal — to have the pleasure, as it were, occur in the saying of the word. Each "pleasure part" should be orchestrated to be different from the last.

The Voice comes from above, and the Woman when she talks to the Voice talks to the sky. The Riverboat Captain is different than the Voice — and the sound comes from the "boat."

PLEASURE CRUISE

WOMAN: This is nice. What a comfortable boat.

MAN: Like a floating living room. Or a big car. Really nice.

WOMAN: I could float like this forever. The sun framed in the sky. The land over there, a safe distance away. Trees bending to the banks of the river. An occasional fisherman. I could float like this forever.

MAN: Me too.

WOMAN: The river is gentle.

MAN: Gentle?

WOMAN: Not rough.

MAN: Smooth ride. I'm going to have a really good time. That is my only hope. Good time.

WOMAN: Comfortable. And the scenery is really . . . nice.

MAN: Couldn't be nicer.

WOMAN: Have you noticed?

MAN: What?

WOMAN: Every question answered. (*She calls out to illustrate, in a sing-song voice.*) "I like coffee I like tea?" How does the rest of it go?

MAN: How about doing me?

WOMAN: Shhh . . .

VOICE: "I like radio and TV." It's an old skipping rhyme. From the 1950s.

MAN: Wow.

WOMAN: I know. Anything we want —

MAN: Does it work for beer?

WOMAN: I don't know.

MAN: *(Calls out.)* Can I get a beer? Please?

VOICE: What kind of beer?

MAN: A cold beer.

(*And a waiter appears, smiling, with a beer.*)

WOMAN: I'd like a beer too.

WAITER: *(Nods.)* Wouldn't you rather have a cold mint julep?

WOMAN: Why yes, I would. Thank you for suggesting a mint julep.

(*Waiter nods and exits.*)

MAN: What a fantastic ride.

WOMAN: I'm going to have fun, too. And maybe get some questions answered. But fun. Fun first. After all, this is a pleasure cruise.

MAN: Did you say "pleasure"?

WOMAN: Pleasure? Yes.

MAN: That word . . . affects me . . . in a . . . mysterious way.

WOMAN: Pleasure . . . yes, I see what you mean. Pleasure.

MAN: Pleasure.

WOMAN: Pleasure.

MAN AND WOMAN TOGETHER: Pleasure!

(A beat.)

MAN: I wonder if I could get some new shoes.

WOMAN: Try it.

MAN: *(Calls out.)* A pair of Nike swervetoppers with aircushion lights. Size 11 and a half.

(A person approaches with new shoes.)

WOMAN: Hi.

(Person doesn't say anything.)

WOMAN: Not everyone is friendly. That's for sure.

Well . . . the river is still gentle. The ride is . . . still nice. I am going to have some . . . fun!

(The waiter appears with her mint julep and a pair of binoculars. Gives both to the woman.)

WOMAN: Thank you. Thank you so much.

Binoculars. How thoughtful.

(Waiter exits.)

WOMAN: Perhaps there are birds. I wonder why else the waiter would give me a pair of binoculars. Perhaps there are . . . birds.

(She puts binoculars up and looks in the sky.)

MAN: *(Calls out.)* Another beer! Please?

WOMAN: *(Still looking.)* No . . . no birds. Huh. Not a bird. I'll keep checking. I've always been interested in birds. What kind of birds populate this part of the world?

MAN: Do you think they heard that I wanted another beer?

VOICE: There are three kinds of birds. Birds of prey, those birds that actually hunt and devour; scavenger birds, the birds that clean up the mess we make; and birds that exist to delight the senses — song birds, birds of beauty.

MAN: Beer?!

WOMAN: *(Calls out.)* Thank you! That was very interesting about the birds.

MAN: I thought you said you were going to have fun.

WOMAN: I am.

MAN: Birds? Not fun.

WOMAN: *(Thinks about it, agrees, decides upon —)* Music!

(Music comes on, and she dances by herself, while the man admires his shoes.)

RIVERBOAT CAPTAIN: THE MUSIC IS TOO LOUD.

WOMAN: What?

RIVERBOAT CAPTAIN: TURN DOWN THE MUSIC. THE MUSIC IS TOO LOUD.

MAN: No! Louder!

(Woman is dancing. A riverboat captain enters and hands the man and a woman a laminated menu. The music cuts off.)

RIVERBOAT CAPTAIN: I'm sorry to inform you. No loud music.

MAN: Why the hell not!

RIVERBOAT CAPTAIN: It's a rule.

WOMAN: Oh. Sorry.

MAN: A rule?

RIVERBOAT CAPTAIN: There are certain rules, yes. As outlined in the literature.

WOMAN: *(Reads.)* Rule #1. No loud music. That's what it says. Sorry.

MAN: What kind of pleasure cruise is this?

WOMAN: Pleasure . . . cruise.

MAN: Pleasure, that word again.

WOMAN: *Pleasure.*

MAN: Pleasure?

WOMAN: Pleasure!

MAN: *(Yawning.)* Pleasure.

(Man is asleep.)

WOMAN: *(Alone.)* I feel . . . lonely.

(She lifts up her binoculars and looks at the banks.)

WOMAN: Oh, I think I see — is that a bird? Is that a . . . ? Goodness. Are those . . . Wolves? Or packs of wild dogs? And I see . . . *(She looks again.)* children . . . hands out . . . are the children hungry? Are the wolves hungry? *(A distant cry from off.)*

WOMAN: Why are you crying, children?

(There is a distant clamor.)

WOMAN: *(To the voice.)* Excuse me. EXCUSE ME. We need to do something about this . . . there seems to be a problem —

VOICE: Yes?

WOMAN: Packs of wild dogs, hungry children — there seems to be a problem on the banks of the river.

VOICE: There is a good safe distance between the boat and the banks. We are surrounded by deep water, with a swift current and there is absolutely no danger here on board —

WOMAN: I don't care about us, I'm worried about them. Bob?

(Man is asleep, he wakes up.)

WOMAN: The children are hungry.

MAN: The CHILDREN!?

WOMAN: Apparently.

MAN: Well, for God's sake, let's feed them.

WOMAN: *(Announces.)* We would like for the children to be fed. Thank you very much for your attention to this matter.

RIVERBOAT CAPTAIN: If I could have your attention, this is your riverboat captain speaking. I'd like to point out that the river is bending. We are now travelling through a BEND in the river. The current here, you will notice, is significantly stronger. We are entering new territory. Please be patient as we navigate through rough water.

MAN: New territory?

WOMAN: I heard, "Rough Water." I don't want to drown.

MAN: He didn't say Rough Water.

WOMAN: I heard "Rough Water."

MAN: Ask.

WOMAN: Excuse me, could you explain what you meant by "Rough Waters"? Hello? Sir? *(Louder.)* Bend in the River? I'd like an explanation, please.

WOMAN: *(To the voice.)* Should we put on our life jackets?

(Silence.)

WOMAN: Before — all our questions — answered.

MAN: I don't know, maybe they were easy questions. I mean, *I* knew the answers.

WOMAN: And so now, when we really need to know the answers, they won't give them to us?

MAN: We could . . . you know . . .

WOMAN: What?

MAN: Take our minds off this part of the ride.

WOMAN: You want to?

MAN: Pleasure.

WOMAN: Pleasure.

MAN: Pleasure.

WOMAN: It's not working.

(Jack enters, bearing a bottle of gin. He's an elegant man.)

WOMAN: Oh good. Hello, kind sir. Perhaps you can help us?

JACK: I can do my best.

WOMAN: We have a few questions and I wonder if you might oblige. We are wondering what the results of the Rough Water will be — seasickness? Will we be sprayed? Should we put our lifejackets on?

JACK: Drink?

MAN: Absolutely.

WOMAN: We were already having fun. I think we were. We were definitely having fun, but then we entered "new territory" and the water became ROUGH.

JACK: Here —

(He offers the bottle.)

WOMAN: Just a little.

MAN: Fill her up!

(The man drinks down a tumbler of gin.)

JACK: Fantastic.

MAN: Hi. I'm Greg. At least I want to be Greg, a guy who is younger and thinner and has a whole lot more going on than Bob. I mean, Bob — what a loser.

JACK: I'm Jack.

WOMAN: His name *is* Bob. It's not GREG —

MAN: Greg for now.

WOMAN: Well if you're Greg, I'm Evelyn . . . a woman of mystery who travels the world and knows the names of all the birds. Evelyn, that's my name.

MAN: Her name is Janet. Give me a break.

WOMAN: You're right. Janet. Never mind. I'd like to be Evelyn, but I'm not sure how —

JACK: I couldn't help but notice how concerned you both are and how oppressive everything has become, so I decided I'd join the party.

WOMAN: Oppressive?

JACK: The scenery, for one.

WOMAN: *(Looks.)* Oh no, not oppressive, it's been surprisingly nice. Goodness. Look at that.

JACK: Industrial wasteland.

MAN: Pour me another!

(Jack does.)

WOMAN: I don't understand. Rolling hills, trees bending down to the water. I remember . . . Now, rubble, piles of rubble and smoke. Strange. I wasn't paying attention. We need to do something. Bob, look beyond —

JACK: Chocolate?

WOMAN: No. Thank you.

JACK: I insist. Chocolate.

(She eats it absentmindedly, then looks through binoculars.)

JACK: *(Looks at woman.)* Pleasure?

WOMAN: *(Wary.)* Pleasure? . . .

JACK: *(More confident.)* Pleasure.

WOMAN: *(Resigned.)* Pleasure.

JACK: *(Jubilant.)* PLEASURE!

MAN: *(To his drink again, softly.)* Pleasure.

(Woman yawns, Jack exits.)

WOMAN: *(To herself.)* I haven't been paying attention.

VOICE: This is a friendly reminder that you are mortal and that you will die, your bones will fall to dust and so will we all. For we are mortal. This is a friendly reminder.

WOMAN: Bob! Bob! BOB!

MAN: What.

WOMAN: Did you hear that? The Voice says we are going to die.

MAN: Holy! You're kidding! Die? We've just started to enjoy ourselves!

VOICE: You are going to die for you are mortal. A Friendly Reminder.

(Woman puts a hat on.)

MAN: What are you doing?

WOMAN: The UV rays are damaging to the skin. We've been out here for a long time. Wrinkles!

(The call of a bird, maybe a cardinal.)

WOMAN: Did you hear a laugh . . . the smallest little chuckle. Someone is laughing at us!

MAN: Relax. No one is laughing at us.

WOMAN: Someone far away thinks we are ridiculous.

MAN: Speak for yourself.

WOMAN: *(Quiet.)* Are we ridiculous?

MAN: I've been sitting here on my tookas. Drinking beer. I disgust myself. I've had enough. *(He stands up.)* Give me those binoculars.

(The woman does.)

MAN: *(Looking.)* Oh. There's someone there. Someone needs help. *(He calls out.)* MAN OVERBOARD!

(Woman takes binoculars.)

WOMAN: Is he drowning? Help, someone, we need some help!

(And the man jumps overboard. A loud splash. The man is gone.)

WOMAN: Bob? Bob — what are you doing! Bob — Help! Someone help!

(She looks through the binoculars.) They're swimming to shore. Should I jump? Excuse me, how do I disembark, how do I get off this boat? I would like to get off this boat! Please?

(Riverboat captain enters.)

RIVERBOAT CAPTAIN: Excuse me. Madam.

WOMAN: Thank Heavens you're here. My companion, my Bob, well he's jumped. Is he going to drown? Am I going to be . . . left alone?

RIVERBOAT CAPTAIN: *(With a flourish.)* Your time with us is over. And so, without further ado, let me present . . . The Bill.

WOMAN: The bill? I have to pay for this?

(Riverboat captain nods.)

WOMAN: Bob, he's got the money. Bob is gone and he's got the — I have to pay for this — *(She opens the bill.)* Do you take credit cards?

VOICE: We take Mastercard, American Express and the Discover card.

WOMAN: *(Relieved.)* All right then.

I can handle this. Credit card . . . Well. Expensive, but . . . credit card. Oh. What a ride. No birds . . . why haven't I seen a bird? *(She looks through the binoculars.)* I think . . . there, oh, blue and the tiniest bit of yellow, small and fast, flying away. A bird, and no one to tell about it. What a beauty!

What's next for us?

Pleasure. Pleasure? Pleasure?

Anyone?

Nothing.

Strange.

Should I stand? Should I sit?

Bob — will you wait for me?

(Awkward.)

One foot here, in front of the other.

(Starting to sing, simply.)

One step, the next step . . .

One foot in front of the other

And soon I'll be walking out the . . . door.

(And the light swallows her up.)

END OF PLAY

PERMISSION ACKNOWLEDGMENTS

Plays for Three or More Actors:

Aimée © 2003 by Erin Blackwell. All inquiries concerning rights, including amateur rights should be addressed to: Erin Blackwell, 939 York Street, San Francisco, CA 94110.

The Roads That Lead Here © 2003 by Lee Blessing. All inquiries concerning rights, including amateur rights should be addressed to: Lee Blessing c/o Judy Boals, Inc. 208 W. 30th St, Ste 401. New York, NY 10001.

Three Dimensions © 2003 by Jerome Hairston. All inquiries concerning rights, including amateur rights should be addressed to: Rosenstone/Wender Attn: Ronald Gwiazda, 38 East 29th Street, New York, NY 10016. (212) 725-9445, fax (212) 725-9447.

Favorite Lady © 2003 by Leanna Renee Hieber. All inquiries concerning rights, including amateur rights should be addressed to: Leanna Hieber, 2066 Tolbert Road, Hamilton, OH 45011.

The Office © 2001 by Kate Hoffower. All inquiries concerning rights, including amateur rights should be addressed to: Kate Hoffower, hufflemonkey@hotmail.com.

Swan Lake Calhoun © 2003 by Yehuda Hyman. All inquiries concerning rights, including amateur rights should be addressed to: Samuel French, Inc., 45 W. 25th St., New York, NY 10010.

Classyass © 2003 by Caleen Sinnette Jennings. All inquiries concerning rights, including amateur rights should be addressed to: Caleen Sinnette Jennings, 7413 Oskaloosa Drive, Derwood, MD 20855.

Airborne © 1997 by Gib Johnson. All inquiries concerning rights, including amateur rights should be addressed to: Gib Johnson, P.O. Box 328, Carpinteria, CA 93014-0328.

The Some of All Parts © 2003 by Mrinalini Kamath. All inquiries concerning rights, including amateur rights should be addressed to: Mrinalini Kamath, mk_writer@yahoo.com.